FRIENDLY FIRE

FRIENDLY FIRE

Accidents in Battle from Ancient Greece to the Gulf War

By
RICHARD TOWNSHEND BICKERS

LEO COOPER

LONDON

First published in Great Britain in 1994 by
LEO COOPER
190 Shaftesbury Avenue, London WC2H 8JL
an imprint of
Pen & Sword Books Ltd,
47 Church Street, Barnsley, South Yorkshire S70 2AS

Copyright © Richard Townshend Bickers, 1994

A CIP catalogue record for this book is available
from the British Library

ISBN 0 85052 372 9

Typeset by Chippendale Ltd, Otley, West Yorkshire

in Linotype Bembo

Printed by
Redwood Books,
Trowbridge,
Wilts.

CONTENTS

ACKNOWLEDGEMENTS

I wish to thank the Royal Air Force Museum, the Imperial War Museum and everyone else who has kindly sent me information about incidents relevant to this book.

Foreword

To the armed forces, 'friendly fire' means being shot at or bombed by one's own side. It is a fatuous term, detested by all, but it serves because everyone understands its meaning. A less injudicious term in use is 'fratricide'. It is inexact because it means the killing of one's brother, but it is reasonable to extend it to include brothers-in-arms. What about sororicide, however, since so many women serve in forward areas? To include them in a masculine category would be careless: not in consideration of 'political correctness' or militant feminist tantrums, but for the sake of accurate language. The most logical term is 'amicide', the killing of friends. 'Blue on blue', adopted by the NATO armed Services, is inoffensive and tactfully covers the whole category.

Every man and, these days, woman who joins a fighting Service has to accept this hazard with the stoicism expressed more than two centuries ago by Isaac Watts – with emphasis on the last line:

> I'll not willingly offend,
> Nor be easily offended;
> What's amiss I'll strive to mend,
> And endure what can't be mended.

For civilians, 'friendly fire' is not only contradictory but also has an ironic or cynical connotation. The term became prominent during the six-day Gulf War in 1991 because, when men were accidentally killed and wounded in this way, the event received unwonted publicity. The narrow scope and short duration of the campaign, and the vast assemblage of reporters close to the scene, were two of the reasons. Sympathy goes to the bereaved families who sought information about why these tragic accidents happened and who was to blame. Also, in this litigious age when claims for compensation are successfully demanded for a multitude of misfortunes that have hitherto been accepted as life's burdens, to be borne with temperance, the indignant outcry was to be expected.

However, as General Schwarzkopf, commanding the United States forces, pointed out, the investigations made by the British and American armed Services involved revealed that it would never be possible to come to a conclusion about blame. 'They happened in every war they've ever had. The difference is they hadn't been reported in the past but they damn sure happened.' Where aircraft were involved, you would have had to be sitting in the cockpit of the aircraft at the time to know exactly what message you received. You would have had to be monitoring the radio on the ground to know exactly what message was sent. 'Someone made a mistake. More than likely more than one person made a mistake. And it resulted in a tragic, terrible loss of life. But why do we have to pursue it? What do we accomplish?'

Military authorities are usually able to conceal these tragedies, to avoid disgrace to the Service or unit that has committed them and protect the feelings of the victims' families. To be killed in action by the enemy is heroic and the grief of the bereaved is tempered with pride. Knowingly to lose a husband, son or brother, wife, daughter or sister through mischance or others' folly is to suffer grief redoubled. Secrecy ensures that the public is unaware how common it is for a sailor, soldier or airman and their female counterparts to be attacked in error by compatriots or allies. These accidents happen on peacetime exercises too.

Friendly fire, or its equivalent before the invention of firearms, dates back to the time when bands of men first assaulted each other. It certainly happened centuries before the birth of Christ, among Roman legionaries in close combat, when a sword-thrust at a foe was dodged, or a slashing stroke deflected by an opponent's shield, and sliced into a comrade.

It was reported in Ancient Greece by Thucydides, writing about the battle fought by night at Epipolae in 413 BC. 'The Athenians now fell into great disorder and perplexity, seeking one another, taking all in front of them for enemies, even though they might be some of their now fleeing friends. They ended by coming into collision with each other in many parts of the field, friends with friends and citizens with citizens. They not only terrified each other but also came to blows and could not be parted.'

In the Middle Ages, English archers were feared for the great range of the arrows they shot from their longbows. English cavalry had a reputation for dash and impetuosity long before the charge of the Light Brigade at Balaclava. In the Hundred Years War, during the Fourteenth and Fifteenth Centuries, there were many times when horsemen charged into the enemy as their own bowmen's flights of arrows came whistling down at the end of their long trajectories and transfixed them.

When bullets, shells or bombs fall on friend instead of foe, incompetence or stupidity is not always the cause. In battle there is confusion of many kinds. The noise of heavy artillery, of shells and bombs exploding, grenades bursting, machine guns and rifles firing; the screams of the wounded, the sight of blood and mutilation; all disorient. These manifestations that stupefy and terrorize happen in the air and at sea as often as they do on land. Changes of weather cause turmoil among ships and aircraft even more than they affect men in foxholes, trenches, gunpits and tanks. In modern warfare, battles are fluid and movements fast; friendly forces become unintentional targets when they are where the enemy is thought to be. Even with radio and field telephones, signals are delayed or misunderstood and communications sometimes fail altogether.

During the Second Battle of Alamein, General Pienaar,

commanding the First South African Division, was provoked to the most cutting brand of sarcasm when he rebuked Desert Air Force for a series of mistaken attacks: 'If you've *got* to bomb my trucks, you might at least hit them! You've missed them every bloody time.'

On the other hand, calamity at war is often the fault of the victim. In the same battle the RAF bombed the 10th Hussars for four hours, for want of a recognition signal, because the recipients of this unwelcome attention did not know what the signal should be.

Misunderstanding and misinterpretation of information are frequent causes of error, the consequences of which are not limited to bombarding one's own troops. A typical instance occurred in a campaign of which the British public was largely ignorant at the time and which is almost unknown to later generations.

When France surrendered to Germany in June, 1940, and 370,397 men of the British Expeditionary Force were evacuated to England, 130,246 French soldiers accompanied them to fight on. The puppet French Government that Germany established at Vichy condemned them and their commander, General de Gaulle, as traitors. Although some members of the French armed forces serving in French colonies and protectorates made for the nearest British-ruled country, to carry on the war against Germany and Italy, the great majority turned their backs on Britain.

In Syria, which had been under French Mandate since 1920, there was a garrison of 45,000 French and Colonial (Algerian and Tunisian) troops and French Air Force squadrons. A British force invaded Syria on 8 June, 1941, and brought the enemy to an armistice on 11 July.

A young Member of Parliament, Lieutenant Somerset de Chair of the Royal Horse Guards, was an Intelligence officer on the Staff of Brigadier J. J. Kingstone, DSO, DFC, a Column Commander. He cited a characteristic – and droll – example of false appreciation that led to waste of flying time, engine hours, petrol and high explosives.

'The Royal Air Force carried air reconnaissance to artistic

lengths and their target maps were a joy to behold. Every important building was numbered with a key at the bottom. They erred only in minor ways – for instance, the *Bordel Militaire de la Campagne* outside Palmyra was listed as a powder magazine and the vicious attempts of our pilots to bomb it were attributed by the French, I learnt later, to jealousy or puritanical instincts.'

One way and another, a lot of banging was going on in and around the resort of pleasure. According to Petronius, 'Delight of lust is gross and brief, And weariness treads on desire.' Blenheims, each delivering four 250lb bombs, must have been even more of a passion-crusher.

This military brothel was not – at that time, anyway – being patronized by the British, so the misjudged attacks on it do not constitute friendly fire. But here is a good specimen of how easily confusion can arise, even when interpreting reconnaissance photographs in an office far from the din and distractions of the battlefield.

In the following pages the book's title has been extended to include calamities that conform to it in essence, although not literally involving the discharge of weapons.

In many instances the names of those involved have been omitted, to avoid causing distress to families and friends.

CHAPTER 1

Fighter Command's most blood-stirring radio codeword was 'Tallyho!'. When given by the leader of a fighter formation, it was the order to attack. When from a leader, or pilot flying alone, to an Operations Controller on the ground, it meant 'Enemy sighted'. 'I am about to attack' was implicit. On the morning of Wednesday 6 September, 1939, it was the prelude to catastrophe.

Royal Air Force units keep a daily account of their activities in the Operations Record Book, more prosaically known as Form 540. The manner in which events are recorded depends on whomever is responsible for the task. There is scope for brevity or prolixity, monotony or vivacity, solemnity or levity.

No 74 (Fighter) Squadron was stationed at Hornchurch, Essex, some two miles east of London's outskirts. Its laconic acknowledgement of the outbreak of the Second World War was the sole entry in its F.540 for Sunday, 3 September, 1939: 'State of War exists between England & Germany.' What about Scotland, Wales and Northern Ireland?

One account of what happened that morning alleges that, immediately on the declaration of war, Fighter Command expected the Germans to attack at once, as they had done to Poland two days earlier. Instant action had also been Hitler's strategy when he invaded Austria in March, 1938, and Czechoslovakia seven months later. Because their area was the closest to Germany, the squadrons in the south-east of England, that version claims, expected to be the first to challenge the Luftwaffe. On the contrary, a 56 Squadron pilot who took part in that morning's events says, 'We were taken by surprise. We were not about to be invaded, like Poland, so weren't expecting instant large-scale air attack.' Moreover, the alarms of the previous three days had all proved false, which emphasized this view.

The first spurious warning was given when air raid sirens sounded in greater London within an hour of the Prime Minister's broadcast at 1115 hrs announcing that Britain had declared war. Fighters were ordered off to intercept an aircraft which, the Observer Corps reported, had crossed the south coast. Neither they nor anti-aircraft units were able to identify it. Before it could be intercepted, it landed at Croydon: where it was found to be a French aeroplane, whose flight plan had not been given, bringing two French officers to join the Allied Air Mission. The sirens signalled 'All Clear' and the fighters were recalled.

The next air raid alarm woke people from their sleep at 0300 hrs the following morning. This time 74 Squadron was called on. Its Operations Record Book reads, 'Six Spitfires of "A" Flight ordered to patrol by sections to intercept enemy raid approaching from Holland. Raid later identified as friendly bomber returning via Felixstowe. Flight ordered to land.' The suspect aircraft was one of several that had flown over Germany that night, dropping propaganda leaflets.

On 5 September there were a couple more false alarms, for which Hurricanes or Spitfires were ordered to scramble (Fighter Command code for 'Take off as quickly as possible'). No 74 was not involved. Its entry for the whole day was, 'Nothing to Record'. (The compiler had an idiosyncratic way with capital letters.)

The brief statement of events on the next day begins: '0645 to 0735. Twelve Spitfire aircraft (6 of "A" Flight and 6 of "B" Flight) ordered to intercept enemy raid . . . '

Every peacetime fighter station covered an area known as its Sector. As the war progressed, smaller airfields nearby were built as satellites to accommodate more squadrons.

The wing commander or group captain commanding the main base was known as the Sector Commander. Each Sector had an Operations Room, which received its orders from the Group Operations Room, from where the tactical use of fighters in several sectors was directed.

The Sector station adjacent to Hornchurch's northern boundary was North Weald, about ten miles due north, which had two Hurricane squadrons, Nos 56 and 151, some of whose aircraft had been scrambled for bogus alarms on the preceding three days. At about 0615 hrs, searchlight batteries informed the duty Controller in the Operations Room at North Weald that high-flying aircraft were over West Mersea, Essex.

Both Sectors were in No 11 Group, whose Headquarters and Operations Room were at Uxbridge. The Group's area extended into Suffolk, Cambridgeshire and Hertfordshire, over the whole of Surrey, Middlesex and Kent, and most of Hampshire. Its Operations Room had also received this information and the duty Controller there ordered North Weald to send one flight (six aircraft) of 56 Squadron to patrol between Harwich and Colchester at 11,000 ft. 'A' Flight was duly ordered off. 'B' Flight was sent up some ten minutes later. It has been stated in some quarters that both flights circled the airfield, forming up, before heading for their patrol line. They did not. The logbook of, and verbal account by, a surviving member of 'B' Flight shows that his flight scrambled some ten minutes after 'A' and they operated separately throughout the sortie.

A squadron's establishment of aircraft was 16, its battle strength 12. Two more pilots, Pilot Officers F. C. 'Tommy' Rose of 'B' Flight and M. L. Hulton-Harrap of 'A' Flight, also went up in two of the four reserve Hurricanes. When 'A' Flight reached the coast, these two were a short distance astern and slightly below. 'B' Flight was approaching the coast, but the other aircraft of 56 Squadron were not yet within its visual range.

By now coastal radar stations and the Observer Corps were reporting several formations off the Thames Estuary.

One of these was 151 Squadron, another was 'A' Flight of 56 Squadron, a third was 56's 'B' Flight and a fourth was the pair from the same squadron that had taken off shortly after 'A' Flight and not caught up.

On the general situation map (also known as the plotting table) at HQ 11 Group, North Weald and Hornchurch, about twenty raids were being plotted. Fifty enemy aircraft were shown near Southend. More fighters were ordered off to intercept the enemy. From North Weald, where there were two Hurricane squadrons, No 151 took off and at no stage did it join up with No 56. From Hornchurch, which had three Spitfire squadrons, No 74 and one flight each of 65 and 54 were ordered up.

In those early days of radar it was difficult to assess the number of aircraft in a formation. Also, the radar crews had not yet had adequate practice, so were unskilled at separating plots.

The Observer Corps was handicapped that morning by mist and, anyway, had been given scant instruction in aircraft recognition. From what little its spotters could see through the haze, therefore, they would have been unable to tell friend from foe, let alone one type of aeroplane from another.

Radio communication was by high frequency single-channel sets. Not only were these subject to much atmospheric disturbance, but also there was no common channel between squadrons or Sectors. Very high frequency four-channel equipment was not introduced until nearly a year later.

Hence, through duplication, lack of training, uncertainty and inadequate communication, came the plethora of allegedly hostile plots. In reality there were no enemy raids over or approaching, and the Controllers at Hornchurch and North Weald were steering their fighter formations towards each other.

The North Weald squadrons were flying directly into the sun, which made it difficult to sight or identify other aircraft or to tell, from long range, whether they were twin-engine or single. They were in the RAF's standard 'V' formation.

One of the best and keenest-sighted pilots and marksmen

in the RAF was leading 151 Squadron: its commander, Squadron Leader E. M. 'Teddy' Donaldson (later Air Commodore CB CBE DSO DFC AFC and credited with 10½ enemy aircraft shot down), had the heartiest laugh in the Service, probably the fiercest moustache and, in 1946, set a new air speed record in a Meteor. He was the first to see a large number of aircraft approaching, but even his remarkable vision could not immediately identify them as Spitfires. However, he decided to make sure before leading his squadron into the attack.

Using the code word for unidentified aircraft, Squadron Leader Donaldson warned his pilots: 'Bogeys twelve o'clock. I think they're friendly. Don't shoot unless positive identification.' So the Spitfires were safe from attack by 151; and the pilots of 56 – who were on a different radio frequency and could not hear this message, anyway – flying separately from their sister North Weald squadron, had not yet seen the Spitfires.

But nobody in 74 Squadron gave a warning that the 'Bandits' were in fact Bogeys and looked like Hurricanes. Yellow Section – three aircraft – of 74's 'A' Flight peeled off and dived into the attack. To fighter pilots eager for battle, the aircraft they had intercepted had to be the enemy. They had been scrambled specifically to shoot down a formation that the control and reporting system had declared was hostile. The orders they were carrying out had emanated from the highest authority concerned, No 11 Group. Their superior officers had taken the decisions and it was their duty to carry them out. The duty Sector Controller had given them certain instructions that had been passed to him by a Group Controller representing the Air Vice Marshal who was Group Commander.

Their targets were the two 56 Squadron Hurricanes that had taken off late and were behind and below the others. These appeared to be escorting the bigger formation – which must therefore be bombers. RAF bomber escorts flew at the same height as, or above, their charges, not below. Never having seen a German bomber force, British fighter pilots were not to know that the Luftwaffe had the same practice.

Luftwaffe fighters flew four abreast and widely spaced, but as yet none had ventured over England, so RAF fighter pilots were not familiar with this formation. These were flying in tight 'Vics' of three, they were small, so unlikely to be bombers, and Essex was too far to be within range of fighters based in Germany. None of this occurred to the attackers.

It is easy to review these factors more than half a century later, in cold blood and from the comfort of an armchair on *terra firma*, with nobody in the vicinity waiting for a chance to shoot at you if you don't get your shot in first. For a young man keyed up for action, in the confines of a cockpit two miles above the ground, with his thumb on a button that could fire a storm of bullets from eight machine guns, and expecting to meet a similar blast in reply, there was no time for ratiocination.

The Hurricane pilots had also been assured that they were going up to meet an enemy raid, but Spitfires with their unique and unmistakable elliptical wings were easier to identify than Hurricanes.

As the Spitfires began shooting, Donaldson told his squadron, 'Do not retaliate, they're friendly.'

No 74 Squadron's Operations Record Book describes with unemotional brevity what ensued. 'F/O Byrne and F/O Freeborn opened fire on two Hurricanes thinking they were hostile. Both Hurricanes were brought down. One pilot, P/O Halton-Harrap, was killed. Other pilot was uninjured. No enemy aircraft were sighted.'

P/O Rose crash-landed, unhurt. He was killed in action over France in May the following year.

It was not until 56 Squadron's 'B' Flight returned to base that they learned that two of their comrades had been shot down by Spitfires.

F/O Byrne and P/O Freeborn were court-martialled, but found 'Not Guilty'. Byrne was shot down over France in May, 1940, and spent the rest of the war as a prisoner.

Freeborn ended the war as a squadron leader with a DFC and 13½ kills to his credit.

The official version of this lethal mistaken identity that the press was allowed to publish read: 'The third warning came at 6.30 a.m., when some German aircraft approached the English coast. Fighters took off and climbed to make an interception, but the enemy aircraft retired. The anti-aircraft gunners mistook the returning fighters for the enemy and opened fire. Londoners standing on the river bridges in Chelsea heard the sound of guns to the east and thought that the German aircraft were over the reaches of the river around Tilbury. Rumour-mongers got busy and averred that a German aeroplane had been brought down near Ongar, in Essex.'

The gossips were partly right. Two aircraft had crashed in Essex, but both were British. One pilot was unharmed, the other had a bullet through his head, fired by a 'friend'.

This appalling misadventure epitomizes the tragic blunders that the words 'friendly fire' suggest to most people.

The mistakes that culminated in an unseemly death can be rationalized as misjudgments bred of a high state of nervous tension, zeal and the determination to meet the enemy and defeat them.

Of the contributing factors, the vagaries of contemporary radar and radio were excusable, poor training of the Observer Corps was not.

Even after nearly a year of war, some pilots had not perfected their aircraft recognition. It was evidently safer to fly a Spitfire, which was the more easily recognizable, than a Hurricane. No 56 Squadron had further proof of this eleven months later. On 11 August, 1940, the squadron took off at 1145 for Rochford, to fly convoy patrols from there. During the first patrol, Sergeant R. D. Baker was seen to be shot down by a Spitfire. A destroyer picked him up, but he was dead.

CHAPTER 2

Soldiers' and sailors' greatest tribulations have not been inflicted by the enemy alone but also by their senior commanders. Airmen of most nations have largely been spared this blight. The aeroplane being a 20th Century invention, flying has from its birth attracted men of enterprise and imagination eager to modernize warfare and give it a new dimension. Its senior officers have, in wartime, been conspicuously younger than their equivalents in the other Services, hence unfettered by outdated dogma.

In Britain, before the 18th Century, commissions were bought or given as a favour. To become an officer needed no military experience: financial means, social position or an influential patron were the instruments. Even when the system was formalized, entrance examinations to the Royal Military Academy at Woolwich (engineers and artillery) or the Royal Military College at Sandhurst (other arms) were of so low a standard that men of lamentably small intelligence could pass them. In the Army, originality was suspect and resented. For a captain, major or colonel to express new ideas in a formal paper or, worse, to write a book, aroused the Generals' anathema and adversely affected his career. The Navy was equally hidebound. A consequence was that most casualties suffered by those who did the fighting were directly or indirectly caused by idiots in high command who made the plans and gave the orders. Those boobies also had a habit of ignoring evidence that did not confirm their preconceptions or conform with their wishes. Their subordinates in the field often concealed such evidence. To reveal the Generals' and Staffs' ignorance or stupidity would hinder their own promotion; it might incur accusations of disloyalty and it could lead to a charge of cowardice.

By the time the Second World War began there was a perceptible improvement in the cleverness shown by Generals. As the war progressed the standard of intelligence rose. Today, with Woolwich and Sandhurst combined as the Royal Military Academy, a stiffer entrance examination, admission open to every social class and a high degree of professional knowledge demanded, there should be fewer damn fools in positions to endanger their comrades' lives. The same optimism applies to the Royal Navy. The Royal Air Force has always required excellence of individual skills – flying an aeroplane to its limits, as the Service insists, is itself a highly skilled craft. The lethal errors that occurred in 1939-1945 were mostly a consequence of the hasty training of amateurs. Those committed by other air forces were merely crass and indicative of their national characteristics.

Before the 18th Century any titled gentleman who wished to raise a regiment or other formation and lead it into battle could offer his services to the Sovereign. In 1642, the seventeenth year of King Charles I's reign, civil war broke out in England when Oliver Cromwell set about abolishing the monarchy and becoming dictator. Noblemen of no military experience took up arms and formed their own contingents on both sides.

One such was a Royalist cavalry commander, George, Baron Goring, aged 34, son of the Earl of Norwich. Well-intentioned though he was, his portrait by Van Dyck gives an unfortunate impression. He is shown three-quarter face, looking to his left and regarding any viewer of the canvas from the corners of his eyes. The effect is to make him appear shifty and sly; which he was. He was also lazy, incompetent, a drunkard and unreliable. To mitigate his unattractive qualities, Edward Hyde, Lord Clarendon, who thus described him in his superb *History of the Great Rebellion*, also wrote of him as 'a man of ready wit and an excellent speaker . . . was like to have most credit with the King in debates'.

Lord Goring was charged with the defence of Portsmouth, 'the strongest and best fortified town then in the kingdom', which lay under siege by Cromwell's men. 'Colonel Goring, though he had sufficient warning and ample supplies to put that place into a posture of defence, had relied too much upon probable and casual assistance, and neglected to do that himself which a vigilant officer would have done.' He was forced to surrender, in return for his and his officers' freedom; a submission that augured his future conduct and the misadventure that qualified him for inclusion here.

Despite his dereliction of duty he was promoted a few months later, by when the major operations had moved to Yorkshire. 'The charge of the horse was at the same time given to General Goring who, by the Queen's favour, notwithstanding all former failings, was recommended to that province and quickly applied himself to action.' He evidently acquitted himself creditably enough, for Clarendon makes no mention of him again until April, 1644, when the Marquis of Newcastle 'sent the body of his horse, under the command of General Goring, to remain in those places he should find most convenient, and from whence he might best infest the enemy'. He evidently conducted this infestation without discredit, as no derogatory comment about him is recorded.

By late summer Goring was in Cornwall and drawing closer to the place where he was destined to bring obloquy on himself again and fatal harm to his troopers. From Beacon Hill, in Cornwall, the King's forces could see all the enemy's dispositions and supply lines. 'Goring was sent, with the greatest part of the horse and fifteen hundred foot, a little westward to St Blazey, to drive the enemy yet closer together, and to cut off the provisions they received from thence.' This was so well executed that they recovered a large area and cut off the main coastal supply point.'

Having acquired some merit, Goring relaxed. An ambush on a Roundhead column was planned that necessitated the destruction of bridges and felling of trees to obstruct the road. 'The notice and orders came to Goring when he was in one of his jovial exercises [a euphemism for debauchery]. He received them with mirth, slighting those who sent them as men who took alarms too warmly, and he continued his delights till all the enemy's horse were passed through his quarters, nor did then pursue them in any time.'

Despite this lapse, the King shortly afterwards accepted the ubiquitous Goring's advice. They were now in the Salisbury area. The King was about to march to Oxford, 'which would have made a fair conclusion of the campaign', with the capture of Donnington Castle and Banbury. Instead, 'a great gaiety possessed Goring, that he earnestly advised the King to march . . . [to] Andover.' Which His Majesty did, with unsatisfactory consequences. Yet the unpredictable Goring redeemed himself the following month at the Battle of Newbury. He was a fool but no coward. Goring, with the Earl of Cleveland's brigade, 'charged them [the enemy] so vigorously that he forced them back in great confusion over a hedge; and, following them over that hedge, was charged by another fresh body, which he defeated likewise, and slew very many of the enemy upon the place,' and pursued the survivors, under heavy fire from their infantry.

Describing Goring's bifarious character, Clarendon praised his courage and 'presentness of mind in danger', but deplored that he could not resist the temptation to drunkenness even when surrounded by the enemy, 'nor would decline it to obtain a victory . . . the most signal misfortunes of his life in war had their rise from that uncontrollable license.' As will be seen, this weakness was also to bring down the most signal misfortune on his men.

Early in 1645 Goring, who was now General of the Horse, was commanding 'a party of horse, foot and dragoons, and a train of artillery' in Hampshire. After a defeat there he retired to Salisbury, where 'his horse committed such horrid outrages and barbarities as they had done in Hampshire without distinction of friends or foes'. Taunton, County Town of Somerset, was in the hands of the Royalists, but the Roundheads were marching on it and Goring's force of

3000 horse and 1500 foot was sent to pursue and prevent them. He failed 'by most supine negligence . . . natural invigilance' and withdrew to Bristol.

Now a large body led by Cromwell and Sir William Waller set out after Goring, who retreated 'far west of Taunton'. Here, 'himself and most of his principal officers took the opportunity to refresh themselves at Exeter, where they stayed three or four days in most scandalous disorder, a great part of his horse living upon free quarter and plundering to the gates of Exeter.'

Towards the end of March, having won a fight against a Cromwellian party, he drew back to Bruton. He submitted a plan to Prince Rupert (the King's German nephew) for an assault on Taunton. Meanwhile 'Lord Goring very gallantly and successfully, by night, fell upon Sir William Waller's quarters twice in less than a week, and killed and took so good a number' that it was estimated that Waller had lost 1000 men. With the remainder of his force, he departed eastwards.

The King wrote to Goring on 11 April, ordering his horse and dragoons to march into Wiltshire and Dorset, while foot and cannon moved directly towards Taunton. Goring replied by 'a short sullen letter' that he had done as ordered and was himself going to Bath to look after his health. 'After some days frolickly spent at Bath he returned to his former temper'; and to duty.

At the end of April Goring was, to his annoyance, ordered by the King to join him at Woodstock, near Oxford. On the way he fell upon two units of enemy cavalry, whom he 'broke and defeated with a great slaughter, which gave him great reputation and made him exceedingly welcome'.

In May he was sent back at the head of his 1500 cavalrymen to join in the attack on Taunton, into which two of Cromwell's infantry units commanded by Sir John Berkeley and Sir John Grenville had forced their way. There, he found the town's enemy garrison 'relieved by a strong party of two thousand horse and three thousand foot, which unhappily arrived at the very instant when the town was being reduced, after the enemy's line had been entered and a third part of the town burned.'

Goring withdrew his force. The column that had raised the siege also moved out and Goring 'fell so opportunely upon their quarters that he did them great mischief'. He also had them trapped now 'between narrow passes that they could neither retire to Taunton nor march eastward' and had them at his mercy.

'But, by the extreme ill disposing of his parties' he led his troopers into the greatest suffering they were to endure.

While, with a third of his command, he maintained vigil over the cornered enemy, he sent two detachments to enter Taunton. That he took advantage of the lull in fighting to indulge in further 'frolickly' self-indulgence is not disclosed but can be assumed. Today one would say that the two parties he ordered forth were inadequately briefed. No reconnaissance was done nor were tactics dictated. Neither detachment was told what the other's orders or plans were.

Riding into Taunton haphazard by different routes, each unaware of the other's whereabouts, they converged. Both, suddenly finding themselves confronted by a body of horsemen, drew sabres and charged. Briefly there was turmoil in the narrow street. Weapons cut and thrust, hooves clattered on the cobblestones, men shouted, wounded horses screamed and tumbled. A trooper, run through from breast to backbone, fell from the saddle. One foot caught in a stirrup and his charger cantered away neighing in terror, dragging his corpse over the cobbles. Another, his arm lopped off above the elbow, blood spurting from the stump, uttered a bellow of rage and spurred his horse headlong into his attacker, whom the force of the impact spilled to the ground, where he was trampled to pulp by a score of pounding hooves. The din in the confined space was amplified by echoes from the walls of buildings on either hand. The air was thick with the tang of sweaty hides, dung and the stench that horses emit when terrified. Troopers fell from the saddle, crying out in agony – among them the two commanders. Then came mutual recognition and bellowed orders from both sides to desist.

Clarendon economically summarized the drama: 'his two parties sent out several ways to fall upon the enemy fell foul on each other, to the loss of many of their men – both the chief officers being dangerously hurt, and one of them taken, before they knew their error.'

The incorrigible Goring, his command reinforced to 5000 foot and 4000 horse, 'grew much more negligent . . . neglected and discouraged his own foot so much that they ran away faster than they could be sent up to him; and gave himself wholly to license.'

He bungled his next attempt to take Taunton and, after further 'entertaining himself in his usual jolity' sailed in October to France, whither King Charles I had sent his heir, Prince Charles, to remain in exile with his mother, Queen Henrietta Maria, in her native land.

On the battlefield, whether literally on the ground or meta-phorically at sea or in the air, men's emotions absorb loss of life and limb without great bitterness; it goes with the job. After a great battle, however, particularly when they have been victorious and euphoria is suddenly invaded by a fatality to a brother-in-arms, the shock is isolated and therefore intense.

In 1808 the Peninsular War broke out and continued for six years. Napoleon Bonaparte had made Joseph, the eldest of his younger brothers, King of Spain. The Spanish people decided to rid themselves of him. Britain took their side and sent an army, commanded by the Duke of Wellington, to fight Napoleon and his 'Frenchies'.

The city of Badajoz was a fortress, an important prize for both sides. The French besieged it and, after many attempts, succeeded in taking it from the Spanish. Wellington, resolved to wrest it from the enemy, laid siege to it on 17 March, 1812, and, on 6 April, stormed and captured it in a feat of arms that ranks as one of the greatest in history.

It had been a hard campaign of long marches, broiling summers and snowbound winters. The battle the British troops had just fought was one of the fiercest they had known. Before they could rest, the weary men had to do what soldiers always have to do – see to their weapons.

Still glowing with the elation of victory, sleepy and near exhaustion, one of them who was cleaning his musket was assailed by a moment of carelessness. The weapon was loaded and his finger touched the trigger. The ball shot a comrade through the head.

The death of one professional soldier was, in comparison with all that had gone before during those three weeks, trivial; but not to the dead soldier's family. To his fellows with whom he had shared a great triumph, it was a tragedy in a way that no mortal wound in action could be counted. To the soldier who killed him, it was a disgrace and a cause for remorse that would torment him all the rest of his days.

The first shots in the Indian Mutiny were fired at Berhampore on 25 February, 1857, by sepoys against their British officers. They lit a fuse that soon ignited similar revolts in other native regiments. The rebellion spread quickly among the civilian population throughout the country, many of whom knew it was imminent. The general uprising collapsed on 25 September with the relief of Lucknow, the capital of Oude, after nearly twelve weeks under siege. Sporadic insurrections continued until March, 1859.

Towards the end of April, indications of disaffection and revolt became apparent at Lucknow. Sir Henry Lawrence, the British Resident or Chief Commissioner of Oude, suppressed the incipient trouble without resorting to violence.

At the first signs of mutiny by the 7th Oude Regiment of irregular infantry, he ordered out the 32nd Foot of the British Army, the 13th, 48th and 71st Native Infantry and 7th Cavalry, who were loyal to the British, and a battery of eight British guns. At dusk he led them to the lines of the 7th Regiment, where a bugler sounded the assembly. When the seditious troops came on parade they found themselves covered by the force that had just arrived.

An eye-witness wrote, 'They were simply ordered to lay down their arms, and they obeyed without a moment's hesitation. At this juncture the port-fires of the artillery were lighted: a sudden panic seized the whole regiment; the men shouted as if frantic, "Do not fire! Do not fire!" and, breaking from their ranks, rushed into their lines for shelter or concealment.'

Sir Henry Lawrence then had the 7th Regiment disbanded and ordered that 'every possible effort should be made to undeceive the sepoys in regard to the pretences upon which their religious prejudices had been awakened'. These were the rumour spread by those who incited mutiny that the new cartridges were greased with a mixture of pig and cow fat which were offensive respectively to Muslims, who abhor the pig as unclean, and Hindus, to whom the cow is sacred.

In May there were again signs of rebellion. On the 31st it erupted with the murder of British officers by native troops and the burning of houses. There was fighting between the loyal and disloyal regiments, which ended with the defeat of the latter. Two miscreants were hanged and eight blown from the guns. All those who had remained steadfast were rewarded with money and some with promotion and special gifts.

The situation deteriorated until, on 29 June, some 8000 insurgents were encamped outside the city. Sir Henry went to meet them with two companies of the British 32nd of Foot, eleven guns and sixty lancers of native Horse. After two hours' fighting and the loss of sixty men, he was forced to retreat.

From 1 July Lucknow lay under siege, with two weeks' provisions and the Residency as the main point of defence. The wives and children of the married officers, other ranks and civilians were sheltering there alongside the garrison that defended them. On the next day an eight-inch shell burst in the Residency and mortally wounded Sir Henry, who died two days later. Night after night the rebels assaulted the huge building and were repulsed. By day they shelled it, causing dreadful wounds and many deaths. Week after week the numbers of the rebels grew. By the eighth week a survivor recalls, 'The report of firearms had become so familiar to the residents that they ceased to notice the missiles as they whistled past their ears'.

Meanwhile Brigadier-General Havelock was on the march with a column to raise the siege. On the night of 24 September it encamped within striking distance. On the following morning Havelock advanced and, after some skirmishes on the way, arrived by nightfall at the palace of Fhureed Baksh, which adjoined the outer wall of the Residency. The General's Staff proposed that the column should halt here for the night, but he considered it too important that the beleaguered garrison should be at once relieved. He ordered the main body of the 78th Highlanders and the Ferozepor Regiment to take the lead in what turned into a desperate hand-to-hand fight in the narrow streets and loopholed passages. If Havelock had delayed it would have been too late: two mines had been driven under the main walls and were about to be detonated.

When, through smoke and flame, the vanguard of the British force had reached a street visible from the Residency, they heard a cheer rise to greet them. To the ears of the defenders came the answering skirl of the bagpipes.

The sentry at the Bailey Guard entrance of the Residency was a loyal sepoy who had endured not only the cannonades and musketry of his own race but also the prospect of torture and slow death at their hands if they were to conquer at the end of the three months' siege.

In the smoke-wreathed gloom of sunset, the triumphant Highlanders mistook him for one of the enemy and shot him.

A senior officer of that era who evinced some of Goring's lack of thorough preparation before an encounter with the enemy was Colonel, later Brigadier-General, R. Walpole. He was known as 'The Old Crimean Lady', an obvious reference to his service three years previously; but whether on account of his age or as a form of the derogatory description 'an old woman' is not known. Either way, such a jibe would raise riots by militant feminists today – some of them in the armed forces.

There were times when, also like Goring, he redeemed himself by a display of good soldiering and – unlike Goring – briskly decisive measures. Official records show that in January, 1858, 'Colonel Walpole, who had been dispatched from Cawnpore to clear Etawah with his column, encountered and defeated the enemy at a place called Akbarpore, where he captured a number of guns and arrested twenty persons of Nana Sahib's immediate retinue, whom he tried for their complicity in that chief's atrocities and immediately hanged. From thence, marching to Mynpoorie and clearing the country as he advanced, he at length joined the Commander-in-Chief at Futteghur.'

On 9 April, 1858, Brigadier-General Walpole left Lucknow at the head of the Lucknow Division, 5000 troops of all arms. Under him was Brigadier Adrian Hope, commanding the infantry. Their purpose was to clear the left bank of the Ganges and secure the passage of the Ramgunga to Aligunge. From there it would join another Division, under the Commander-in-Chief, and continue to Bareilly, a total distance of 156 miles.

The few roads that existed in India were tracks made by bullock carts, horses and travellers on foot. In the country that the column had to cross there was none. During the Hot Weather it was usual to make night marches, when it was comparatively cool. This was impracticable in that district, where the column must avoid the numerous dangers and difficulties that beset its route on every side. These were not only topographical but also posed by ambuscades and hostile strongholds. Moving the heavy guns was another awkward business, owing to the terrain, and too precarious in the dark. In consequence, officers and men were exposed to the sun's great heat and many 'sank under its scorching influence'.

Reveillé every day was at 3 a.m., tents were struck, a light breakfast was eaten and the Division moved off at 5 a.m. The Commander-in-Chief had recommended to Walpole that he should halt by 8 a.m., but the column marched daily until nine and on 11 April did not halt until ten. On that morning many reported sick from fatigue and exposure to the sun.

It was hoped that by resting at night the troops might reach Bareilly in about twelve days, before the Rains, which began in May and caused the rivers to flood and spread all over the countryside in every direction. There was, therefore, no time to spare for minor encounters with the enemy and certainly none to waste on laying siege to any stronghold, which might also be attended by serious casualties. Walpole knew it, but succumbed to temptation.

For the first two days the Division met no obstruction from the enemy. On 12 April he wrote to the Chief of Staff: 'At Ruheemebad I destroyed a fort which was being constructed, which belonged to Soobah Sing . . . said to be the head of 4000 men; he commanded two regiments at Lucknow, where he fought against us.' This was the first squandering of time.

On 15 April the column came to a jungle fort hidden by trees and undergrowth, a place of little importance near a village called Roodamow or Rooya.

An officer of the Highland Brigade who was present described events in a letter dated 23 April. 'We marched with a sort of indefinite expectation of meeting the enemy, based on the reports that had lately reached us. An advance guard of Companies 1, 2 and 3 of the 42nd Royal Highlanders, under the command of Major Wilkinson, preceded the main column, which was headed by the 42nd Royal Highlanders left in front. Firing was heard, I think, about half-past nine: the fort of Rooya could be seen in some parts embosomed amid trees.'

In his despatch of 16 April to the Chief of Staff, Walpole gave this account: 'Nurput Sing, who I stated in my despatch of yesterday was at Rooya fort, did not come in or send any satisfactory reply to the message of Captain Thurburn, the magistrate, who accompanies this force. I therefore thought it advisable to attack him, particularly as Captain Thurburn informed me that he understood that his intentions were certainly hostile to the government.'

He intended to enter the fort by 'getting round to the north side, which was stated to be the weakest part, where there was a gate, and where there were very few guns.'

He did not reveal who had given him this information or why he placed total reliance on it. The inference must be that it was merely hearsay. One of the oldest military precepts is 'Time spent on reconnaissance is never wasted'. Walpole, on hearsay evidence, committed the unforgivable transgression of failing to reconnoitre the objective before sending his troops in.

His despatch continued: 'The fort on the east and north side is almost surrounded with jungle, and at these two sides the only two gates were stated to be [hearsay again]. It is a large oblong [in fact, it was hexagonal – Walpole evidently never examined it, even after the fight], with numerous circular bastions all round it, pierced for guns, and loopholes for musketry, and surrounded by a broad and deep ditch: there is an inner fort or citadel, surrounded in like manner by a deep ditch, and with a high wall considerably elevated above the rest of the work. On the west and part of the south side there was a large piece of water, which was partially dried up.' It sounds architecturally imposing as well as forbidding; but although it was murderously difficult to assault, particularly without reconnaissance, it was built of mud.

The officer of Highlanders already quoted gave details in his letter. 'No 10 Company 42nd Royal Highlanders was ordered to go out skirmishing in front of horse artillery guns, with No 9 in support. About 300 yards from the fort, Nos 7 and 8 were sent up to Brigadier-General Walpole in front of the guns, and were ordered by him to skirmish without support, and to advance until they came within sight of the gate of the fort, and to open fire.' It is clear that Walpole did not brief his officers about his plan, for: 'It was supposed by those concerned that this movement was for the purpose of preventing the rebels in the fort from escaping by the gate referred to [he means the north], and that Major Wilkinson would make an attack on the weak side [he means the east, but Walpole believed the north gate to be the weaker] and that the rebels, driven before him would naturally think of leaving the fort by the gate [north].'

To revert to Walpole's despatch. Having moved to the north side and sent some of his infantry forward: 'a heavy fire of musketry was immediately opened upon them, and an occasional gun; the cavalry at the same time swept entirely round to the west side, to cut off all communication with the fort. A tolerable view of the fort having been obtained from the road which leads into it from the north [the first glimpse of the target, as there had been no reconnaissance], the heavy guns were brought up; the two 18-pounders were placed on it; the two 8-inch mortars behind a wood still further to the right.

'After a short time a great many of the infantry were killed and wounded from having crept up too near the fort, from which the fire of rifles and matchlocks was very heavy: these men had gone much nearer to the fort than I wished or intended them to go.'

But he had not given them precise orders. Nor was the killing done only by the enemy. Suddenly there was the rush of wind and the soughing sound of cannonballs. Loud curses rose from the men trapped in the great ditch as their comrades fell, or with their own dying breaths as they themselves were torn asunder. The friendly cannonballs were overshooting the fort and dropping among the attackers who were going round the south side of the fort to reach the west.

A captain brought word to Brigadier Adrian Hope of this and of the shambles in the broad, deep ditch. There, without scaling ladders, the British and Indian troops were unable to climb up to the wall of the fort. They were under withering fire from above and being slaughtered by the dozen. Hope informed Walpole of the friendly cannonfire and the way in which troops were trapped in the ditch with neither shelter nor means of egress. Walpole would not believe the report, a classic example of the self-delusion exhibited by Generals of his era. Hope therefore rode around the south side of the fort to the west, to see for himself.

The same Highland officer wrote: 'I dare say he thought that everything that morning had been dreadfully mismanaged. Before he had been a minute on the perilous ground, he was shot.' The bullet went through his neck, shoulder and lung. Another officer who was at the scene recorded, 'Hope said, "They have done for me; remember me to my friends;" and died in a few seconds.'

Walpole admitted in his despatch that, 'By half-past two that afternoon it was clear that the artillery had made little or no impression upon the place', so he decided to withdraw to the south for the night and assault 'the south-east angle on the following morning'.

When morning came, a reconnaissance at last found that the enemy had evacuated the fort. Walpole's despatch claimed that the numbers of the enemy varied so much that it was 'impossible to arrive at any certainty upon that point; but I am inclined to think that . . . about 1500 to be nearly correct'.

The truth was that there were between 300 and 400 men in the fort, most of whom were unarmed villagers.

This whole unseemly escapade cost the Lucknow Division 120 casualties, more of them killed than wounded. Friendly fire accounted for a large part of those.

CHAPTER 3

To anyone with some knowledge of American history or of
the 'Wild West', the name of Custer recalls at once his battle
with the Sioux in which he died. 'Custer's Last Stand' beside
the Little Bighorn River is one of the most greatly honoured
acts of fortitude in the annals of the old West. There is much
more for which to remember and admire him. He was a
natural leader, he was brave far beyond the courage that
anyone must have who chooses a military career; he was
intelligent and he had affection and respect for his comrades
of all ranks because they had chosen a life of danger and
hardship. A lifelong teetotaller and non-smoker, his greatest
pleasures were fighting and hunting.

A fault he shared with General Walpole was that he drove
his men and horses too hard; but whereas 'The Old Crimean
Lady' did so because he was thick-headed and callous, it was
zeal that impelled General Custer. It was also selfishness:
not only was he blessed with unusual stamina, but also
while his troopers rode coarse remounts his own horses were
thoroughbreds, which gave them much greater endurance
– 'more bottom' in horsemen's parlance. He insisted that
cavalry could be of maximum use only if it moved swiftly.
His ruthless forcing of the pace meant that every formation he
commanded covered greater distances, faster, than any other,
which often took Confederate cavalry and Indian tribes by
surprise.

George Armstrong Custer was born on 5 December, 1839.

His father and grandfather were blacksmiths, but young George's ambitions lay higher. In the small town in which he grew up, education was offered only to the age of sixteen. He must have been exceptionally intelligent, for when he finished his he taught at the school for two years before entering the United States Military Academy at West Point. His four years there earned him one of the worst records ever: his sloppy drill, slovenly dress, inattention to study and lack of discipline thrice almost brought him expulsion. He was saved only by his superlative horsemanship. When he passed out in July, 1861, bottom of his class of 34, he joined the cavalry. Immediately he was put in authority over others he became a keen disciplinarian and a meticulous professional fighting commander.

The Civil War had begun three months earlier and he fought in its first great battle, at Bull Run. Here he witnessed the disintegration of morale, the inability of officers to control either their men or themselves and the abandonment of pride, which has so often assailed troops the first time they are in action and led by officers as raw as they.

It was literally a display of 'blue on blue', for that was the colour of the Union Army's uniform. It was 'grey on grey' too, the hue that the Confederate force wore. In a favourite phrase of contemporary journalese, 'death had taken its frightful toll' to an extent that persuaded the participants on both sides to heed the dubious maxim that discretion is the better part of valour. They abandoned themselves to disorder. Some Union regiments wore a shade of pale blue that could be taken for grey. Some of the rebel units wore a shade of grey that bordered on blue. Unable clearly to discern friend from foe, both North and South, the liberators and the practitioners of slavery, aimed their muskets and cannon at any human form that might be about to do the same to them. Hundreds were felled by their own comrades.

Soon conspicuous for his leadership and reckless courage, Custer was promoted in June, 1863, from lieutenant to Brigadier-General of Volunteers. At once, his appearance changed – he became impeccably dressed and flamboyant. Six feet tall, with fair shoulder-length hair, broad-shouldered and slim, he designed his own uniform to set off his handsome physique and features. Army kitchens were no longer acceptable: even on campaign he employed his own cook, always a woman. He commanded a cavalry brigade at Gettysburg and every important battle that followed. His brother Thomas, six years his junior, had enlisted at the outbreak of war and now, commissioned, was his *aide de camp*. At the age of twenty he was made a lieutenant-colonel of Volunteers.

When peace came, in 1866, Custer was reduced to captain, but General Sheridan, under whom he had served, soon had him promoted to lieutenant-colonel commanding the newly formed Seventh Cavalry. Thomas also joined the Regiment.

Fully to understand Custer's attitude to the Indians, his methods of fighting them, his treatment of his own men and why he again became involved in friendly fire, it is necessary to learn something of the enemy's nature and tactics. Whatever their tribe, they knew intimately every feature of the great areas over which they constantly roamed. They wandered purposefully, hunting buffaloes – of whose hides they made their clothes and tents and whose flesh they ate – deer and other game. They hunted horses to catch and train and sought fresh grazing and water, hills and woodland to shelter their camps in the winter.

They were treacherous and no race was more cruel. Their numbers were small, so they had to perfect the skills of guerrilla warfare and are believed to have killed ten Americans for every warrior they lost. It was not only against soldiers whom they made war: they attacked isolated farmsteads and the way stations along the stage coach trails staffed at the most by six men. Cutler described the scene of one slaughter: 'I discovered the bodies of the three station-keepers, so mangled and burned as to be scarcely recognizable as human beings. They were scalped and horribly disfigured.'

Soon after, at another place, a father, mother and their five children, the eldest a daughter of eighteen, were returning in their wagon one evening from a visit to friends. A band of Kiowas, led by their Chief, Satanta, attacked them and killed the father and one child, both of whom they scalped. They bound the survivors and put them on horses before setting off for their village hundreds of miles away. They let the mother carry her youngest child, a baby. During the night it began to cry. Fearing that it might be heard by pursuers, one of the Indians dragged it from her and bashed its brains out against a tree. The Indians kept their captives for a year until they were ransomed. The eldest daughter had been passed around to be ravaged. The smallest, a girl, cried so much that the Indians scorched the soles of her feet until the flesh was burned away.

A lieutenant, ten troopers and their guide, a friendly Sioux Chief named Red Bead, bringing despatches to Custer, were attacked by Sioux. When their bodies were found, all had been scalped and their skulls smashed. They had been so mutilated that only the Indian was recognizable. The sinews of their arms and legs had been cut, they had been tortured by fire, their noses were hacked off and their faces further disfigured. Every body was pierced by twenty to fifty arrows, which remained in them.

Shortly after, a trooper was captured in an action against mounted Indians. During one of the frequent short periods of peace, those who had tortured this prisoner described to Custer what they had done to him, 'with consummate coolness and particularity of detail'. It is clear from the readiness with which Indians would talk about their atrocities that they felt no guilt; to them it was routine and the treatment they expected to receive if taken prisoner by an enemy tribe. 'He was tied to a stake, strips of flesh cut from his body, arms and legs, burning brands thrust into the bleeding wounds, the nose, lips and ears cut off, and finally, when from loss of blood, excessive pain, and anguish, the poor, bleeding, almost senseless mortal fell to the ground exhausted, the younger Indians were permitted to rush in and despatch him with their knives.'

Seeing for themselves the Indians' barbarity, or hearing of it from others who had witnessed their inventive cruelty, was the incentive for soldiers to shoot when in doubt, at the risk of hitting comrades.

The Army blamed the Indian Bureau, which was staffed by civil agents with misguided sympathies and traders who had no conscience about selling arms to anyone. Custer commented on the official statement of the Commissioner of Indian Affairs in 1867: 'The Indian Bureau not only did not deny the accusations, but went so far as to claim that all our difficulties with the Indians could be traced to the fact that the military commanders had forbidden the traders from furnishing the Indians with arms and ammunition. It was rather a queer complaint on which to justify a war that, because the Government would not furnish the savages with implements for murdering its subjects in approved modern method, these same savages would therefore reluctantly be forced to murder and scalp such settlers and travellers as fell in their paths, in the old fashioned tomahawk, bow and arrow style.'

He also describes a meeting between an Army delegation led by a General, and an Indian one led by several tribal Chiefs. The Indians were all armed with lances, bows and quivers full of barbed arrows. Each also carried a hunting knife and tomahawk. Everyone of them 'was supplied with either a breech-loading rifle or revolver, sometimes with both – the latter obtained through the wise foresight and strong love of fair play which prevails in the Indian Department, which, seeing that its wards are determined to fight, is equally determined that there shall be no advantage taken, but that the two sides shall be armed alike with the latest improved style of breech-loaders. The only difference is that the soldier, if he loses his weapon, is charged double price for it; while to avoid making any such charge against the Indian, his weapons are given him without conditions attached.'

The heavy sarcasm was justified in its protest against the deluded liberal attitudes that have since permeated the whole world and destroyed a just morality based on discipline and retribution.

The end of the Civil War was immediately followed by a

resurgence of Indian depredations. In an attack on Fort Phil Kearney the entire garrison of three officers and ninety-one other ranks was killed. In the spring of 1867 operations against the Indians were begun under the command of Major-General Hancock. At dawn on 15 April Custer set off in command of eight troops of cavalry to hunt a large force of Sioux.

After many days of rising at first light and riding at a forced pace until dark, always alert for an ambush by day or attack by night, knowing what merciless brutality they would suffer if they fell into enemy hands, everyone's nerves were raw and reactions swift. One afternoon Custer's command marched from sunrise until 2 p.m., rested for five hours, then resumed its way. Late that night it bivouacked. An hour later, at daybreak, a sentry gave the alarm: 'Indians!'

Custer detailed men to make sure the horses would not stampede and led the rest on foot through the mist to a place from which they could scan the landscape. About a mile away, mounted figures became visible. This was not the untidy concourse of a tribe, men, women and children, on the move. The horsemen were approaching in orderly formation, looking determined and hostile. Custer ordered his force into defence positions. The advancing riders stopped and a few detached themselves from the rest to ride forward, as though to reconnoitre. Tired after their long march, ill-tempered at being roused from so short a sleep, restless at the prospect of an attack by an enemy whose numbers they had not been able to assess, the cavalry were baffled when the outriders suddenly turned, rejoined the main body and the whole lot wheeled about and trotted away.

Two officers and a section of troopers mounted and charged after them, firing from the saddle. In the poor light, their aim unsteady as they galloped over the uneven ground with their targets barely within range, they saw no-one fall. The 'enemy' turned to face them once more. Voices called: not with the blood-curdling whoops of Indians on the warpath, but in English.

The suspected attackers were a detachment of cavalry who

had lost their way. Custer used a bell-tent whose shape they had mistaken for a wigwam, which had roused their commander's suspicions. They were withdrawing to try to encircle the camp when Custer sent a detail in pursuit.

The next time Custer opened fire on his own kith, it was no accident.

Among the rank and file, many were becoming disillusioned about the quality of army life. They had volunteered for what they believed was a noble calling. Patriotism, comradeship, romantic notions about the wilds and the glamour of a cavalry charge; pride in their manhood – skill at arms, the toughness to endure hard living, the guts to face a brave and remorseless enemy: all had attracted them to their uniform. Their expectations were mostly fulfilled, but for some the rigorous conditions of field service, discovery of the reality that wounds more often brought death than recovery, the poor food and low pay outweighed any satisfaction they found in service under the flag.

Dishonest contractors hundreds of miles from any battle-field made fortunes. Crates supposedly containing tinned rations would be packed with bricks. Canned meat would often be gristle, fat and bone, far below the quality for which the Commissariat Department had paid. Bread and biscuits would be mouldy and infested by weevils. On campaign in country where game was scarce, diet was so sparse it would hardly sustain a child.

In the region where Custer's regiment was in barracks there was another temptation to lure men into breaking the oath they had taken on enlistment: gold had been found. Deserters were stealing away to earn quick and comparatively easy wealth.

One morning, when Custer's regiment was to leave at dawn on a long march deep into Indian territory, over forty men were found to have gone missing during the night. The regiment moved off but covered only fifteen miles before halting. The men supposed that they were to spend the night here, but it was only to rest and graze the horses. When, unexpectedly, the march was resumed, sixteen troopers who had evidently planned to desert after dark were seen hurrying back the way they had come. Seven of them were mounted and got away. The nine on foot ran for it but were overhauled.

Custer's report claimed that the major leading the pursuers called on them several times to surrender, but was ignored. It alleges that one of them fired at the pursuers, who then responded and shot down three. According to him, the remaining six were captured and allowed to resume duty.

That any were spared is not credible. When men began to disappear from barracks, Custer had ordered that no deserters were to be brought back alive. He hated deserters as deeply as he despised them, because they depleted a force's strength and therefore endangered their comrades. It was also a form of cowardice, a failing he would never condone. He was not the sort of man to tolerate any latitude in the interpretation of orders. It is thought that his inflexible discipline, as well as his forced marches, was responsible for many of the desertions.

From the prairies of North America to eastern France and the Franco-Prussian War of 1870-71. It was a war deliberately created by chicanery, a warning of the suffering and destruction that Germany was to inflict on Europe through the same unsavoury inherent characteristic in 1914 and again in 1939.

The seed of this war was sown by the selection of a German prince as King of Spain, to which France's ruler, Napoleon III, objected. Prince Bismarck, Chief Minister to the King of Prussia, Wilhelm I, precipitated the consequence of this conflict of views by altering and publishing a telegram which made it appear that the King of Prussia had insulted the French Ambassador.

Today, such an incident would be accepted as the normally boorish behaviour to which international diplomacy has degenerated. In those days it was an insupportable offence against honour. On 19 June, 1870, France declared war. The Prussians, with their allies Bavaria and other German states, invaded France at three points and on 6 August the main armies came in contact. Soon the French had to abandon

Alsace-Lorraine, except for the fortress of Metz.

The dangers of battle and the bitterness of defeat drove many officers and men to the fighting man's usual means of relieving stress and fear – the bottle. A certain young company commander named Masson imbibed too well; his aim was erratic when he fired his pistol, so instead of taking out a ravaging Prussian, he despatched his own sergeant major.

Now the scene moves to the Eastern Mediterranean and from Custer's quick, skilful decisiveness and Masson's remedy for battle fatigue, to the ponderous ineptitude of a dolt.

In the Nineteenth Century the British Army and Royal Navy were graced with Generals such as Wellington, Campbell and Roberts, Admirals of the calibre of Nelson, Hardy and Fisher, but burdened also with a preponderance of dimwits in these high offices.

That naval officers of those days tended to be unimaginative was the consequence of entering the Service in early adolescence. They were immediately subjected to harsh discipline and a training that produced automatons rather than men of initiative. The dignity and authority of rank was instilled in them to the extent that their conditioned reflexes in response to an order were as robotic as Pavlov's dogs to the sound of a bell. A ship's captain ate in his private dining cabin. Other officers, down to the rank of lieutenant, had their meals and could spend their leisure in the wardroom. Sublieutenants and midshipmen messed in the gunroom. The latter were called 'snotties' because they wore brass buttons on their cuffs, allegedly to prevent them wiping their noses there. They were firmly kept in their place in a unique way, for no such humiliation was practised in the Army, although very junior officers were ignored by their seniors. If a midshipman committed a misdemeanour the First Lieutenant sent him to the senior sublieutenant, who gave him six strokes with a dirk scabbard. When the Royal Naval College at Dartmouth was founded in 1905, cadets were admitted at 13 and joined the Fleet four years later – at an age when public schoolboys are usually spared the indignity of corporal punishment.

The exaggerated distinctions in status produced a rank-consciousness that inhibited officers from venturing to draw their superiors' attention to an impending calamity. Actually to suggest a course of action to avoid it would have been regarded by both as a gross breach of discipline, tradition and manners. To rescind an order of one's own would be to admit having made an unsound decision in the first place – an intolerable implication of inefficiency.

In 1893 the Mediterranean Fleet was exercising off the Levantine coast, near Beirut. Admiral Tryon, in command, was on the bridge of his flagship, *Victoria*, watching his fleet, in columns of two divisions steaming in line ahead, the columns separated by 3600 feet (six cable lengths). He gave the order for them to reverse direction by turning inwards. It was obvious to the Flag Captain and every other officer and rating on the bridge, and on board *Camperdown*, opposite to her in the parallel line, that there was not enough separation between the two files of vessels for these two big ships to do this without colliding. Unless Tryon's eyes were as dim as his brain proved to be, he must have known that there was not sea room enough to perform the manoeuvre.

Neither the Captain nor the fleet's Second-in-Command, Rear-Admiral Markham, dared to draw Tryon's attention to this. Nor would Tryon lower his dignity by countermanding his order. Neither Captain of the ships involved dared request permission to belay the order. They knew that their ships' combined radii of turn exceeded the distance that separated them. Everyone above decks, officers and ratings, watched as *Camperdown* and *Victoria* bore down on each other.

Camperdown struck *Victoria* amidships and sent her to the bottom. Twenty-two officers and 337 ratings died, among them Admiral Tryon.

There is an eerie corollary to this exhibition of cussedness and waste of lives. Lady Tryon claimed to have seen an apparition of her husband at an hour of the day that, she learned soon after, coincided with her husband's death.

CHAPTER 4

The Boer War – 1899–1902 – provided some bizarre material for the study of the erratic behaviour and retarded intellect so often evident among officers holding the highest appointments. The British Commander-in-Chief, General Sir Redvers Buller, who had won the Victoria Cross in the Zulu War of 1879 as the dashing leader of irregular cavalry, was a star performer in the rôle of a man promoted beyond his ability. He had already seen active service in China, Canada, Ashanti and Sudan. By the time he took command in South Africa he was sixty years old and perhaps too mentally and physically fatigued for the task after years of campaigning in tropical climates. In fact, he died only eight years later.

In appearance he was the epitome of the martial hero – 'a fine figure of a man', in the hackneyed phrase to which his equally unimaginative admirers resorted. He might well have inspired Sir W. S. Gilbert's line, 'the very model of a modern Major-General'. A contemporary described him fulsomely: 'There is no stronger commander in the British Army than this remote, almost grimly resolute and completely independent, utterly fearless, steadfast and vigorous man. Big-boned, square-jawed, strong-minded, strong-headed.' The same admirer praised his smartness, sagacity and administrative capacity and declared that 'He was born to be a soldier of the very best English type, needless to say the best type of all.'

Stephanus Johannes Paulus Kruger – 'Oom (Uncle) Paul'

– President of the Transvaal and a rebel against the British since 1880, described Buller more succinctly: 'He was fat and double-chinned.'

Buller had spent ten years at the War Office immediately before being appointed Commander-in-Chief of the British Expeditionary Force to South Africa. Lord Lansdowne, who became Foreign Secretary in 1900, said that Buller confided in him, 'I have always considered that I was better as second in a complex military affair than as officer in chief command. I have never been in a position where the whole load of responsibility fell on me.'

There is pathos in this confession by so brave a man who was conscious that he lacked singleness of purpose, was irresolute, indecisive and had little faith in the plans he made. He was not without a degree of low cunning, for when 'the whole load of responsibility' did fall on him, in South Africa, he smartly passed the buck. He shifted on to his subordinates the responsibility that he should have carried, by setting them tasks without any instructions on how to set about them. They were left to get on with the fighting as they saw fit and when their tactics went awry he was able to disclaim all blame.

It was his bad luck that most of the Generals on to whom he off-loaded the burdens he should have borne were no brighter than he was. One of his Divisional Commanders was Major-General Lord Methuen, who went to Eton at about the time that Buller left. Neither did much to justify that other Old Etonian, Wellington's, assertion that the Battle of Waterloo was won on the playing fields of this distinguished school. Indeed, Redvers Buller was so often a loser that his troops called him 'Reverse' Buller and Methuen, given the opportunity, made a conspicuous fool of himself.

Buller sent Methuen, with a force of 8,000, to attack the 3,000 Boers who held the Modder River. Like Walpole at Fort Rooyah, when the objective came in sight he did not bother to reconnoitre it. Assuming that as he could see no enemy troops, there was none there, he ordered his command to make a frontal attack across the flat veldt.

In doing so, he ignored two basic principles dictated by Field-Marshal Lord Roberts of Kandahar, the greatest soldier of the time. The first duty of a commander is reconnaissance; and modern weapons make frontal attacks over open ground impossible.

The Boers, hidden by the steep near-side riverbank, waited until their attackers were within close range before opening fire. Hundreds of British troops fell. Those who were not hit went down voluntarily and were unable to advance or retreat. They and the wounded lay all day under the sun in a temperature of 110 degrees.

Methuen ordered his artillery into action. Any shells that did not go harmlessly over the enemy's heads fell among the British. When darkness fell, he withdrew his infantry, leaving 500 dead and wounded. How many were killed or injured by their own gunners has never been revealed. The Boers lost three men.

Another clown let loose with the lives of thousands of men in his hands was one of the obscurer Generals, Gatacre. At the Battle of Stromberg Junction he made a night march, intending to attack at dawn. He had neglected to study the route on a map and when his column was well on its way he found that he had forgotten to bring anyone who did know how to get to the objective.

When the sun rose he was astonished to see ahead of him a range of hills that should have been behind. Totally disoriented, he positioned his troops facing the wrong way. The Boers opened fire on their backs. Gatacre endured this for half an hour, then pulled his men out. On reaching his start line of the previous night, he thought he had done well to get back with only ninety casualties. It was only then that a count showed he had left 600 men behind because he had forgotten to pass the order to retreat to them.

He did not actually turn his own guns on his own men, but his imbecilic behaviour in handing 600 of them over to the enemy amounted to much the same dereliction.

★   ★   ★

The Great War of 1914–18 was prolific in self-destructive incidents. One of the most tragic occurred on the ill-judged expedition to Gallipoli, where grotesque optimism about the pulverizing effect of naval bombardments and ignorance of the terrain when troops were put ashore led to disaster.

It is difficult to credit that the most senior commanders of the Royal Navy and the Army, and their Staffs, had the crass notion that the Turks could be defeated from the sea alone, without an invasion of the land. Aerial photography had been made since 1884, when cameras were fitted to free balloons, and was now being done by aeroplanes on the Western Front. No photographic reconnaissance, however, had been made over the Gallipoli peninsula, nor had there been any opportunity for scouts to reconnoitre the terrain. Nobody in the War Office or Admiralty therefore had any notion of how favourable the peninsula was to defence. Nor had anyone the commonsense to realize that wars cannot be won without infantry. However much a landscape is battered by shells and bombs, the final assault has to be made by riflemen. The absurd plan of those who directed war operations from London was for naval cannonades alone to hammer the Turks into submission.

To appreciate the enormity of the two events that qualify this phase of the war for inclusion in this record of fatal errors, a knowledge of relevant detail in the total scope of this grisly misadventure is necessary.

At the northern end of Turkey's west coast there is an entry, two miles wide, to the Dardanelles, a strip of water 41 miles long and about four wide at its broadest, leading to the Sea of Marmara, which covers some 100 miles by fifty. The Gallipoli peninsula forms the Dardanelles' northern shore. Constantinople (now Istanbul) is on its north side, where the narrow Bosphorus Strait gives admittance to the Black Sea.

For many years Britain had been on good terms with Turkey and was building two Dreadnought battleships for the Turkish Navy, but the relationship had been deteriorating: Turkey wanted to borrow money, Britain refused to lend it and cancelled the shipbuilding contract. Germany lent Turkey the money.

On 4 August, 1914, Britain declared war on Germany, which was already at war with France and Russia. On the same day, the Germans secretly formed an alliance with the Turks and gave them a battleship and a cruiser.

On 1 November Britain declared war on Turkey. Strategically, that country was important because from there Egypt, which was a British Protectorate, could be attacked. If Egypt fell, Britain would lose use of the Suez Canal, essential for quick passage between Britain and her Asian empire. Persia and the Persian Gulf, where Britain had oil interests, would also be endangered.

Two days later, two British cruisers bombarded forts on the Gallipoli side of the Dardanelles, where there were extensive minefields, while two French battleships shelled the opposite shore. The British ships steamed parallel to the coast and at extreme range, 13,000 yards offshore. According to an officer on board one of His Majesty's ships, the eighty rounds they expended did little damage apart from destroying a magazine. After this fatuous day's work aggression was suspended while the next move was argued in London. Bombardments were resumed in February and March, 1915.

There were two opposing strategic theories. The British General Staff, the French Government and French High Command believed that the decisive battles would have to be fought in France. Winston Churchill, First Lord of the Admiralty, and Admiral Lord 'Jacky' Fisher, the First Sea Lord, said that it would be impossible to break through the German lines in France and that victory would be won only by attacking in the Near East – which could bring in Italy and the Balkan countries as allies. Field-Marshal Lord Kitchener, the Secretary for War, decided that no troops were available for a venture in the Levant.

On 2 January, 1915, the Russian forces in the Caucasus came under heavy attacks by the Turks. Russia asked its allies for action against these. The Dardanelles was selected as the only effective place to attack. By now, the need for a strong ground force was recognized.

The huge British fleet sent there comprised six battleships, two battle cruisers, several cruisers and destroyers and the first seaplane carrier built for the Royal Navy, the *Ark Royal*. France sent four battleships. This whole armada bombarded the defences of the Dardanelles on 18 March. The ground forces came from the British, Australian, New Zealand, Indian and French Armies. The first landings were made on 25 April.

By 7 August, after months of heavy losses from enemy action and dysentery, the invaders were confronted by the necessity to capture a dominant feature, Sari Bair (Yellow Ridge). This was two miles long and nearly 1000 feet high on which there were three hilltops, each of about 850 feet, separated from each other by some half a mile. The most southerly one was Chunuk Bair.

The assault throughout had been made difficult by the terrain, which was bare hillside where gullies and rocks formed natural fortifications. The slopes were steep, the troops were burdened with heavy loads of equipment, weary from days and nights of fighting, weakened by short rations, bemused by the broiling sun.

On 8 August, after some of the hardest fighting of the whole war, the New Zealanders captured Chunuk Bair. The preliminary naval bombardment had wrought havoc among the Turks, who were lying in shallow trenches – they could scoop only a few inches out of the rocky soil. All day the victorious New Zealanders, in the abandoned Turkish trenches on the crest, and the Gloucesters, who were with them, were under heavy fire. The Gloucesters suffered so many casualties that they were forced to retire. Reinforcements could not reach the New Zealanders and by early evening the trenches were so choked with dead that they also had to withdraw. Throughout the day, the most forward troops were so close to the enemy that they had been discomfited by the machine-gun and rifle fire of their comrades in support and shell bursts from their own artillery.

At 5 p.m. a warship opened fire on Chunuk Bair and shrapnel flew among the New Zealanders with dreadful effect. They had survived a hellish twelve hours of exposure to sunstroke, the ricochet of large fragments of rock chipped off by their own supporting riflemen and machine-gunners, and of thirst aggravated by the dust that mingled with cordite fumes. Now they were on the verge of sundown and temporary relief, but the wretchedness of the daylight hours was not yet over. With more dead and wounded all around him, an officer managed to send a message by field telephone and eventually the shelling stopped. By then only two men were left alive in his trench. Of 700 New Zealanders who had attacked Chunuk Bair at first light, only 70 of those left alive were unwounded. The Welsh Fusiliers lost 417 and the Gloucesters all their officers and sergeants and 350 other ranks.

The official records make no mention of the shelling by a friendly naval vessel, nor is it known how many of the above casualties this inflicted.

The battle was not over yet – nor was the misdirected friendly fire.

When darkness fell, naval searchlights lit the ridge to keep the Turks pinned down while rifle and automatic fire went on throughout the night. The 1/6 Gurkhas had gone up to join the New Zealanders. At dawn on 9 August ships put down a barrage on the enemy positions. Shells fell so close to the men waiting to attack that they were dazzled by the flashes and almost suffocated by the fumes. The bombardment was supposed to stop at 5.15 a.m., but continued until 5.20. The officer commanding the Gurkhas waited three minutes to ensure that the shelling was over – so he thought – before leading his men in a charge. The attack went in with bayonets and kukris. Officers emptied their revolvers into the enemy, then used them as clubs. The men clubbed with their rifle butts. The battle cry of the Gurkhas rose above the groans and cries of the wounded and dying. The Turks turned and scuttled down the far hillside.

The pursuing Gurkhas, British and New Zealanders heard

the boom of large-calibre naval armament echo among the crags.

The lieutenant-colonel commanding a detachment of Warwicks and South Lancashires described what happened next. 'We had gone about 300 feet down when . . . suddenly our own Navy put six twelve-inch monitor shells into us, and all was terrible confusion . . . It was an appalling sight . . . the place was a mass of blood and limbs and screams.'

Among those killed were 100 Gurkhas.

In December, the campaign was abandoned and by 8 January, 1916, the last Allied troops were embarked.

In France, being fired on by mistake by those who thought they were shooting at Germans was an occupational hazard from the outset. Every day and every night both sides suffered from the same kinds of accidents. Patrols returning across no-man's-land in the dark would be mistaken for the enemy by nervous sentries and welcomed with rifle bullets or grenades. During an attack, infantry would advance faster than expected and their own artillery barrage would fall on them. Guards escorting prisoners would be machine-gunned because their own troops had not been able to pick them out among the enemy uniforms. The Somme, Loos, Ypres, Passchendaele – whose name has become synonymous with devastation and should not be pronounced 'Passion-dale', which incongruously suggests bucolic lust, but 'Pahss-khen-dah-le' – all were scenes of these commonest of tragedies.

In the Battle of Loos, which began on 25 September, 1915, and ended on 13 October, another threat was let loose – gas. Only native English-speakers, with their general contempt for the correct pronunciation of foreign languages, would see a pun there. In Dutch and Flemish, a double-o is pronounced like the 'o' in 'cote'.

Robert Graves, known to the present public – if at all – from a television adaptation of his *I Claudius*, not as a poet, was an infantry officer who fought at Loos. A line he wrote, 'His eyes are quickened so with grief', might have been inspired there.

The purpose of the battle was to recover Lens and the surrounding coal mines from the Germans. His regiment went into the line on 19 September, during the preliminary bombardment of the German trenches. The British shared involuntarily at the receiving end. 'We had more casualties from our own shorts and blow-backs [rounds exploding in the breech] than from German shells. Much of the ammunition that our batteries were using came from America and contained a high percentage of duds; the driving-bands were always coming off. We had fifty casualties in the ranks and three officer casualties. This was before steel helmets were issued; we would not have lost nearly so many if we had had them.'

The Allies were to use gas, in emulation of the Germans, for the first time. The written orders began, 'The attack will be preceded by forty minutes discharge of the accessory, which will clear the path for a thousand yards, so that the two railway lines will be occupied without difficulty.' 'Accessory' was the code for gas. The intention was to keep it secret, but French civilians knew all about it long before this. The orders continued: 'Owing to the strength of the accessory, men should be warned against remaining too long in captured trenches where the accessory is likely to collect, but to keep to the open and above all to push on. It is important that if smoke-helmets have to be pulled down they must be tucked in under the shirt.'

Graves's Company Commander, a regular officer known as The Actor, thought poorly of chemical warfare. 'It's damnable. It's not soldiering to use stuff like that even though the Germans did start it. It's dirty and it'll bring us bad luck. We're sure to bungle it. Look at those new gas companies – sorry, I mean accessory companies. Their very look makes me tremble. Chemistry dons from London University, a few lads straight from school, one or two NCOs of the old-soldier type, trained together for three weeks, then given a job as responsible as this. Of course they'll bungle it. How could they do anything else? But let's be merry. I'm going on again.'

That was not the only legitimate cause of apprehension. Their objective for the first day's attack was La Bassée. Another Company Commander pointed out that, two centuries earlier, the Duke of Marlborough had known better than to make a frontal attack on the La Bassée lines and had gone round them.

At a bibulous dinner in mess on the night before the battle, a divisional staff officer was heard to confide to a friend, about their Divisional Commander, 'See that silly old woman over there? Calls himself General Commanding. Doesn't know where he is; doesn't know where his division is; can't read a map properly. He's marched the poor sods off their feet and left his supplies behind, God knows where. They've had to use their iron rations and what they could pick up in the villages. And tomorrow he's going to fight a battle. Doesn't know anything about battles; the men have never been in trenches before, and tomorrow's going to be a glorious balls-up, and the day after tomorrow he'll be sent home.'

The following midnight, after a twenty-mile march, Graves's battalion moved into trench sidings, cold and tired. It was raining. At dawn the British bombardment opened. The enemy responded. Shells fell on the British front line, then the men in the sidings heard rifle and machine-gun fire. Wounded men came stumbling past. Many of them were yellow-faced and choking – nobody waiting to go into the front trench knew why. Graves says, ' "What's happened? What's happened?" I asked. "Bloody balls-up" was the most detailed answer.'

Customarily before an attack a double tot of rum was issued to all ranks. The Actor grew impatient. 'Where the bloody hell's that storeman gone?'

The company fixed bayonets. Orders came to move up to the front line. Still no rum. At that moment the storeman appeared. 'He was hugging a rum bottle, without rifle or equipment, red-faced and retching.' He had been gassed, but nobody knew that yet. 'He staggered up to The Actor and said: "There you are, sir," then fell on his face in the thick mud of the sump-pit at the junction of the trench and the siding.'

The stopper flew out and the three gallons of rum gushed out on to the ground.

'The Actor said nothing. It was a crime deserving the death penalty.' He put one foot on the foreman's neck, the other in the small of his back, and trod him into the mud. Then he gave the order 'Company Forward'. The company marched off to the front-line trench. Their boots trampled the recumbent body, 'and that was the last heard of the storeman'.

The gas-choked wretch would probably have preferred a quick, clean death from a bullet fired by one of his mates.

Graves learned what the 'bloody balls-up' had been when the company reached the trench. At 4.30 a.m., the gas company's commander telephoned Divisional Headquarters to report: 'Dead calm. Impossible discharge accessory'. The bold desk warriors of the Staff, far from the line, replied, 'Accessory to be discharged at all costs'. That the costs would be British lives does not seem to have occurred to them. Even if it had, there are precedents from that war to suggest that they would not have cared greatly.

The officer who had predicted that the gas company would prove incompetent was right. The spanners for unscrewing the cocks of the cylinders were found, with few exceptions, to be of the wrong sizes. Men dashed up and down the trench, borrowing tools. When they managed to release some of the gas, it formed a dense cloud a few yards ahead, then drifted back over the British trenches.

The Germans, warned by the bombardment that an attack was imminent, had put on their gas helmets – which were much more efficient than the British ones. German shells began to fall among the infantry who were waiting to make the assault. These burst open several more gas cylinders and more poisonous, choking fumes suffused the trench. 'The gas company,' Graves records, 'dispersed.'

Two companies of the Middlesex Regiment opened the attack. They found that the British artillery had not yet shelled the wire and were virtually wiped out. Two other companies rushed back to the support line, to get away from the gas, and attacked from there. The barbed wire in front of the support trench, which was the old front line, had not been removed. These troops were thus also entangled in 'friendly wire' and machine-gunned.

Portugal is proud of its claim to be Britain's oldest ally. When Portuguese troops were first put in the front line, Brigadier-General F. P. Crozier, CB, CMG, DSO, was unimpressed by the way the High Command had positioned them.

His brigade arrived in the line south of Armentières on the night of 7–8 April. He did not 'like the feel of things'. On walking 700 yards along the Portuguese front with one of his colonels, he found that his forebodings were justified. Writing in the historic present, he recorded, 'We examine rifles and ammunition lying about. All are rusty and useless. The bombs are the same.' He wondered where the men were. 'A snore gives me my answer. Practically all the front line sleeps heavily and bootless in cubby holes covered with waterproof sheets.' His comment, 'This is a pretty mess,' was admirably restrained.

His companion remarked that the trenches were 'fearfully bad' because stretchers could not move with ease in them.

The Brigadier agreed, said he would see what could be done about it and added, less than encouragingly, 'I should think we'll be shot up out of this at dawn, via the rear.'

On returning to his headquarters, he telephoned the British Mission attached to the Portuguese. The officer to whom he spoke told him, 'They're always like that.'

'They shouldn't be there,' Crozier retorted. 'That's the crime.'

Early on the morning of 9 April, the bombardment woke him. His batman gave him his respirator and he set off for his command post. His description of what followed is laconic. 'All is mystery and gas . . . the Portuguese bolt and leave the way open to the Germans.' His prediction about the direction from which the enemy would come was right: 'Stonewall Metcalfe, "at rest" in billets is the first in action in rear of our position.'

The Brigade's flank was exposed. During that day, and the three following, the Germans made ground in a series of close-quarter encounters with grave casualties on both sides.

Brigadier Crozier summarized, 'It has been a ghastly let down, but a triumph for certain individuals [among the British, who won richly deserved decorations]. If the Portuguese had never entered the line it would not have been so.'

His troops had been ordered to 'fire at all field grey advancing towards us'. The Portuguese as well as the Germans wore this colour. 'Hundreds of Portuguese were mown down by our machine-guns and rifle fire.'

Asked where the fault for this 'mishap' lay, he asserted, 'Undoubtedly with the military higher command, for permitting the Channel Ports and England, to say nothing of the valuable lives of British soldiers, to be risked. Political considerations may necessitate certain lines of action which may be distasteful to the soldier; but the safety of the line is far above political considerations or expediency.'

General Headquarters maintained that they did not know the Portuguese divisions were so inferior, about which excuse he comments, 'Neither they nor their mission could have known the difference between a bad soldier and a good one.'

Someone accused him of being unkind to the Portuguese. Rightly, he would not have this. 'I think GHQ was unkind to them for ever putting them in such a position: they must have known all about them. They caused them to be slaughtered, and they lost us many lives.'

The essential weakness in those particular allies was, as it most often is, that they were badly led. The Duke of Wellington had found them adequate when led by British officers.

That was an event that could be described as killing by default, since the British troops were not specifically warned that the Portuguese wore the same colour uniform as the enemy.

There were also acts of deliberate shooting at 'friends'. In 1916 an Irish regiment was once so incensed when a West Country battalion panicked and ran that it did not hesitate to turn its fire on the Englishmen before giving its attention to the advancing Germans.

This was not a unique reaction in scorn for cowardice, nor was its opposite, a hatred and fear of rash bravery. Officers or NCOs in the habit of leading men into mortal danger when it could honourably have been avoided were often shot by one of them – and will be in the future. It happened, and not seldom, in the Great War and in every major war since. The 'gong-happy' who were bent on winning decorations were often disliked and even feared, rather than admired, by those who had to soldier, sail or fly with them. The same went for the preternaturally aggressive who met every situation by hurling themselves into violent action without pausing to consider whether there were other means of meeting it effectively. American soldiers coined the expressive adjective 'gung-ho' to describe them, with distaste for that style of leadership as much as with admiration for its courage.

Another provocation to deliver friendly fire, which has occurred in every war since 1914, is surrender at the last minute. Battle makes men angry and excited. When they finally over-run an enemy position that has been stubbornly defended for a long time and have seen great numbers of their friends killed, they do not feel like sparing those who have done it. When they have fought their way to within a few yards of the defenders, and these then drop their weapons and emerge from a trench, foxhole or ruined building with their hands up, or wave white flags, the attackers are in no mood to accept the plea for mercy. The soldier thinks, 'They've been trying to kill me for the past several hours, and they were still at it a minute ago. They stopped only because they knew we'd beaten them. To hell with them.' And he shoots as he exclaims, 'Too late, mate'.

When surrender is accepted after a bitter fight at close

quarters, it is not always unanimous. Those who are determined to exact retribution will turn their weapons on the vanquished, careless of how many of their own fellows have the misfortune also to be in the bullets' path.

It happens no less frequently that when troops in the very forefront of the battle line offer surrender, those behind them shoot them in the back. This is sometimes from regimental pride. Sometimes it is for self-preservation: if the men in the most forward positions give in, those in support are faced with an even smaller chance of survival than they had expected. On the killing ground, practicality rules, not sentiment or pity.

In 1914 aeroplanes were still a strange sight to most people. It was only eleven years since Wilbur and Orville Wright had made man's first flights in a heavier than air machine. In the Italo-Turkish war of 1911 the Italians had sent nine aeroplanes to Libya, where the Turks ruled. The next year, when Bulgaria, Greece and Montenegro together went to war against the Turks in Macedonia, the Bulgarians sent a handful of flying machines to the front. But it was not until the Great War that large-scale air operations began. Neither the British, French nor German ground troops were able to identify their own aircraft or the enemy's: often, their airmen could not either. Both sides used them for reconnaissance, which meant flying at a height that was within rifle range. Consequently, Royal Flying Corps, Aviation Militaire and Luftstreitkräfte pilots and observers were frequently fired at by their compatriots or allies.

Rifle fire was not a great menace, because it was difficult to judge the right amount of deflection to allow for a target moving at sixty to eighty miles an hour. Nevertheless, only six days after the RFC arrived in France, aeroplanes began to return from their sorties with 'friendly' bullet holes in them. The first RFC pilot to complain that his machine had been hit by British troops was a lieutenant who was proud of his moustache. 'Some blasted Tommy fired at me from the flank. Bullet went through the lower wing, across the cockpit and out through the upper wing. Damn nearly shaved me – felt the hot wind on my face.' Fired at head-on or from astern, when no deflection was needed, he would have been lucky to escape with his life.

Machine guns were a much more dangerous gauntlet to run, because they could saturate several cubic yards of air space in an aeroplane's flight path and thus score lucky hits if it held its course and flew into them. Anti-aircraft cannon, whose shell bursts scattered hundreds of fragments, were of course the greatest danger. Two days after the bewhiskered pilot's narrow squeak, the pilot and observer of a BE2 who strayed over the French sector of the front line found their aircraft hurled thirty feet up by the blast of a French anti-aircraft shell, turned on to its back and more than twenty holes torn in its fuselage by splinters.

Charles Nungesser, the most colourful, reckless and eccentric member of l'Aviation Militaire, shot down forty-five German aircraft, the third-highest French score. He had reached a total of six when, in 1916, a British pilot nearly ended his fighting career. It caused him particular chagrin because he had gone to great pains to ensure that his aeroplane was easily recognizable. In defiance of superstition and morbidity, he had had a skull and crossbones, a coffin, two lighted candles and a black heart painted on it in addition to the conventional markings.

He was patrolling at 6000 ft in his Nieuport, scanning the sky for enemy aircraft, when he spotted a Sopwith half a kilometre away and a couple of hundred metres above. He did not worry about it and turned his gaze elsewhere. Half a minute later bullets were making holes in the Nieuport's fuselage behind the cockpit. A quick half-roll and dive, a sharp climb with a roll off the top saved his life. By the time he was able to settle down again, his attacker had gone: presumably having discovered his mistake. On landing, Nungesser had a huge red, white and blue 'V' painted on his upper wing for the benefit of any other allies who were not aware of his macabre personal insignia.

The second highest scoring French pilot, Georges Guynemer, with fifty-three victories, had little in common with Charles Nungesser except that they were both targets for British pilots' bullets. Whereas Nungesser was a boxer, horseman and swimming champion with a sturdy physique and a fondness for pretty women that was ardently reciprocated, Guynemer was sickly-looking and ascetic. He had been suspected of having tuberculosis as a boy and twice failed his medical examination before finally being allowed to join the air force.

On 23 September, 1916, flying over Epertigny, he went to the rescue of Lieutenant Renaud de la Fregolière, a fellow Spad pilot, and shot down the Fokker with which he was engaged. Five minutes later he shot down another. A third Fokker went down under his gun five minutes after that. Having resumed his patrol in good spirits, he was rudely reminded that there was often something lacking in the accuracy with which ground troops identified aeroplanes. A shell from a French anti-aircraft battery hit one of his wings and sent him spiralling steeply down. The aircraft was out of control, landed heavily and broke up. The official account of it reported that, 'The pilot emerged from the wreckage miraculously alive, with only minor injuries. It was his eighteenth victory.'

On 20 August, 1917, Capitaine Guynemer was patrolling in his Spad (Société Pour l'Aviation et ses Dérivées) single-seater near Poperinghe when he spotted a Deutsche Flugzeug Werke C1, a two-seater in which the observer, armed with a Parabellum machine gun, occupied the front cockpit. The disparity in performance between the two aircraft was wide: the German capable of less than 100 mph, the French with a top speed of 133 mph. Making a high quarter attack, where the enemy gunner could not aim at him, Guynemer shot the DFW down – his fifty-third success. On the way home he was taken by surprise when the pilot of a Royal Flying Corps Camel, the most successful fighter of the war, mistook him for a German and fired at him. Bullets severed two of the Spad's longerons before the British pilot realized his mistake.

A few days after this Guynemer took command of Les Cigognes, the most famous French squadron. Administrative duties prevented him from flying for nearly three weeks. On 11 September he took off on a patrol from which he did not return.

CHAPTER 5

From the onset of the Second World War, the Luftwaffe did not confine its attacks and reconnaissances to southern England. The whole country had its share and Scotland received almost daily attention for the first twelve months.

No 602 (City of Glasgow) Squadron of the Auxiliary Air Force was one of Britain's most active and successful defenders. Its efficiency was paid a high compliment when, in May, 1939, it converted from Gladiators to Spitfires before most regular squadrons received them. It was in action for the first time in October of that year and shot down the first enemy aircraft to fall on British soil.

Before the squadron won this distinction, however, there was one false alarm. On a misty, cloudy autumn morning a section of three aircraft was on patrol off the coast of Fife when the leader saw a twin-engined aircraft diving through the foggy wraiths. The section accelerated in pursuit and, just before the unidentified aircraft disappeared into cloud, the leader fired a ranging burst. It was impossible to tell whether he had hit it, but confirmation was awaiting the section when it returned to base.

A less than complimentary message had been telephoned from Dyce, where an Anson had landed with its fuselage riddled with bullet holes. The squadron had committed an embarrassing 'clanger', but, as one of its members, Findlay Boyd – of whom more will be heard later – said, 'It was damn good long-range shooting'.

On 29 December a section was ordered off to intercept a bomber formation reported over North Berwick at 1000 ft. One of the three pilots was Archie McKellar, who had brought down the Heinkel 111 that was the first to fall in Britain. (Before he was killed in November, 1940, he scored twenty-one confirmed victories and won a DSO, DFC and bar.) The control and reporting system had declared the formation to be definitely hostile, so as soon as it came in sight the section opened fire. In the sea mist, the slim-fuselaged bombers looked like Dornier 17s ('Flying Pencils'). The Hampden bomber also had a slim fuselage, and that is what these were. After their first pass the fighter pilots realized their mistake, but recognition came too late for two of the Hampdens. Those of their crews who had not been killed by their 'friends' drowned in the cold North Sea.

To make the situation more uncomfortable, the surviving Hampdens did not have enough fuel left to reach their base, so had to spend the night at Drem, where their assailants were stationed. The next morning, 602's pilots were woken by the sound of bombers flying low over them. The officers' mess had been totally stripped of lavatory rolls – which were being duly returned by the bombers.

By 1939 the size of the belligerents' air forces added a huge new dimension to the risks of friendly fire. In the Great War, the bombing of targets far behind the lines on both sides had seldom put civilians or one's own troops at risk and it was rare for ground fire to be aimed at friendly aircraft. The Royal Flying Corps' targets were mostly railway junctions, ammunition dumps and vehicle parks. Ground strafing, which began seriously in 1916, was almost all directed at the trenches, not in close support of advancing troops. British infantry did on occasions wear, for pilots' and observers' benefit, identifying marks on their backs when they 'went over the top', but this was not to protect them from attack by the RFC or, after April, 1918, the RAF: it was to enable reconnaissance and artillery spotting aeroplanes to report their positions to headquarters and the guns.

By the time the Second Great War that everyone had been expecting for the past twelve months broke out, Britain's air raid precautions had been well publicized. Newspapers and cinema news reels showed air raid wardens, rescue squads, fire and medical services rehearsing. The population accepted them as a normal part of everyday wartime life. Each man, woman and child in the country had been issued with a gasmask that had always to be carried. Air raid shelters and the signs pointing to them were already a familiar sight.

It was not always gunfire or bombs that caused fatalities to compatriots. The first unexpected type of accident of the new war occurred on Sunday 25 February, 1940, when pupil pilots were on night flying training at Croydon. A Blenheim that failed to become airborne at the end of its take-off run crashed into a semi-detached house whose back garden adjoined the airfield. It killed the lady and her daughter who lived there.

There was one particular hazard to which the RAF had quickly to become inured. Fighter pilots and Bomber and Coastal Command crews soon met it when crossing back over the British coast after a sortie out to sea. The anti-aircraft gunners were diligently alert for the enemy, but their aircraft recognition did not always match their enthusiasm. Being shot at by friendly coastal batteries became as unremarkable as skidding on a banana skin or a hangover after a heavy night in the mess.

It was not confined to the shore gun sites either. Jim 'Ginger' Lacey, then a sergeant and destined to be the RAF's top-scoring pilot in the Battle of Britain, had a tale to tell about what he characteristically described as 'rather an amusing incident'. To appreciate it, one has to have some idea of what sort of young man Ginger was. To describe him as imperturbable and a total stranger to the display of emotion – 'laid back', in current idiom – was to say only the half of it. He was probably the calmest and least demonstrative man in the Service.

In late July, 1940, when the Battle of Britain was a couple of weeks old, his Hurricane squadron (501) was stationed at

Middle Wallop, in Hampshire. He had already shot down five enemy aircraft while operating in France and five more since returning to England. Every night some fighter pilots were on night flying detail. There were no purpose-designed night fighters then and experimental airborne radar was in its infancy and not yet in squadron service. Day fighter pilots, vectored (given a course to steer) by ground controllers towards real or suspected enemy aircraft shown on the Ops Room plotting table, had to prowl the dark skies straining their eyes for a glimpse of a German bomber's exhaust flames or its silhouette against the moon or stars.

Sergeant J. H. Lacey, DFM, having been sent in a dozen different directions one night, was pleased to see a Heinkel 111 caught in the beams of several searchlights a couple of miles ahead and a trifle above. As soon as he started to climb towards it, some of the searchlights switched to him. At any moment now the ack-ack guns would open up at him unless he could prove he was on their side. Single-engine pilots identified themselves by flashing the Letters of the Day on their downward lights, multi-engine crews by firing the Colours of the Day from a Verey pistol.

A moment's thought brought the correct letters to Lacey's mind and he duly signalled them. Immediately after, he saw a red and then a green Verey light burst above the Heinkel. He was amazed when the searchlights that were still holding the bomber, which he knew was hostile, shifted their beams on to him. Ten seconds later, the anti-aircraft gunners let fly at the Hurricane. Blinded by the searchlights and taking evasive action amid a cluster of shell bursts, he lost sight of his target.

When he landed, he found that the time was well past midnight, the hour at which the Letters and Colours of the Day changed. He had flashed the wrong identification letters and the Germans had fired the right colours. Whether it was superb Intelligence or sheer fluke that had saved the Jerries' skins was to remain a mystery.

At about this time another fighter pilot marked out for great fame was the main actor in a night flying encounter that was by no means 'rather amusing'. Flight Lieutenant

Robert Tuck, DFC, a Flight Commander on 92 (Spitfire) Squadron, had shot down six German aeroplanes and shared in a seventh, before his squadron was posted to a quiet sector in Wales.

On a wet but moonlit night he was chasing a Junkers 88 that was making its way from one patch of cloud to another while he tried to get close enough to shoot at it. Ginger Lacey was an exceptional pilot and an exceptional shot. Bob Tuck was only an average pilot but he was at least as good a shot as Ginger. When, for a few seconds, the Ju88 had to break cover he took his chance and got in a quick burst. He thought he had hit it and this was confirmed when he saw it dump its bombload and turn away from its original course, which was towards Cardiff and Swansea, obviously going home. Tuck did not have enough fuel left to close the range and try again, so he had to return to base.

The following morning he had a telephone call from his father to say that his sister's husband, a soldier, had been killed during the night when a bomb fell on his barrack hut at a small place in South Wales.

A few minutes' enquiry by the Squadron Intelligence Officer revealed that this was one of the bombs that Bob Tuck had frightened the Ju88 pilot into jettisoning.

The first twelve months of the war were as rich as any with vexations on land, at sea and in the air, of the kind that prompted Sir John Betjeman's verse 'In Westminster Abbey'; although forgiveness was not much in evidence. Stoical acceptance was all.

> Gracious Lord, oh bomb the Germans.
> Spare their women for Thy Sake,
> And if that is not too easy
> We will pardon Thy mistake.
> But, gracious Lord, whate'er shall be
> Don't let anyone bomb me.

It is time to revert to the Syrian and Iraqi deserts, where the force (Kingcol) commanded by Brigadier Kingstone, who was thought by many to be the best fighting Brigadier in the Army, was making its way towards Baghdad. This was a diversion from its main task, which was to secure Lebanon and Syria.

It was a picturesque assembly, flavoured with a touch of romance that was absent from other theatres of war. The Life Guards and Royal Horse Guards were there, alongside eight RAF armoured cars that had come straight from fighting in the deserts of Egypt and Libya. So were the Arab Legion, formed and commanded in Jordan by Major-General J. B. Glubb, DSO, OBE, MC. Although the ultimate objective was the defeat of the Vichy French army and air force in Syria, there was also some business to attend to first in Iraq. In this, Kingcol was joined by the King's Own Royal Regiment, the Essex Regiment and the Assyrian Levies, between whom and the Iraqis smouldered an ancient and inextinguishable hatred. The British contingent had landed in Palestine (now Israel) and was bound for Baghdad, city of Haroun Al Rashid, of the Arabian Nights and the glittering dome and minarets of the magnificent Blue Mosque at Khadimain. A tough and dangerous 600-mile desert journey faced them and Kingstone's command was to be the first conquering army ever to cross from the Mediterranean to the Tigris.

In 1914 Britain had sent an Indian Army force to Mesopotamia, as Iraq was then called, to protect her Persian Gulf oilfields. Its first act was to capture Basra. Mesopotamia had been under Turkish rule for two centuries and the Turks poured troops in to meet the invasion. A gruelling campaign ensued, which ended in March, 1917, with a British victory and capture of Baghdad.

In 1919 the Kingdom of Iraq was formed and became a British protectorate. Under its mandate, Britain had been training and equipping the Iraqi Army and training Iraqi pilots in England for some twenty years. Predictably, the Iraqis felt that the time had come to rule themselves in total independence for a change. With Britain heavily engaged in a renewed war against Germany, they seized their chance. British subjects were interned in the compound of the British Embassy, while the Iraqi Army laid siege to the RAF station at Habbaniyah, 55 miles west of the capital, where there were a few Gladiator fighters and Blenheim bombers.

Kingstone's column had reached the Euphrates and was almost on the last lap of its race to Baghdad. Patrols – lorried infantry, or cavalry in an infantry rôle, sometimes accompanied by an RAF armoured car – were sent out in sundry directions. One was ordered to reconnoitre around the lake at Habbaniyah (home of an enthusiastic RAF sailing club, but there were no boats out that day).

Communication between air and ground proved to be imperfect. As their lorry bumped over the sands, whose monotony would presently be relieved by the sight of a sheet of water ninety square miles in area, Household Cavalry troopers commanded by a lieutenant spotted a sturdy biplane approaching. To identify it, there was no need to wait until it came close enough to see its markings: it was plainly a Gladiator. They hoped it would alleviate their boredom by the sort of amiable gesture that the RAF usually accorded its friends: a slow roll or an Immelmann, with luck an 'upward Charlie' climbing roll or even two, perhaps a dive and low pass while the pilot rocked his wings in cheerful salutation.

The Gladiator dived, sure enough. Tracer bullets coruscated in the air that shimmered from the heat of an almost vertical sun. The sound of the lorry's engine was drowned by the roar of the fighter's 840hp Mercury and bursts from its four machine guns. Sand spurted up around the lorry where bullets were thudding into the ground as the driver swung the steering wheel from side to side to dodge them.

One of the troopers tumbled off his seat, killed by a bullet through his neck.

A few days later there was another unpalatable incident. The Royal Engineers were building a bridge for the column across the Abu Guraib canal. Squadron Leader Cassano, who commanded the RAF armoured cars, approached the canal bank on foot at a point where a private of the Essex Regiment was on guard. He was startled to hear a rifle shot and the hum of a bullet past his ear.

His response, an admirable display of British coolness under fire, could hardly have been what the trigger-happy sentry expected. 'I may look like a Wog,' Cassano told him, 'but I am not, and you ought to be court martialled for missing me at fifteen yards.'

And now to sea. The evacuation of the British Expeditionary Force from France between 26 May and 4 June, 1940, saw many accidental killings and maimings of allies as they crossed the Channel. On a moonless night, with E-boats as always on the hunt, the minesweeper *Lydd* was on her way back from her third trip to Dunkirk. She was packed with 250 British and French troops. Ahead of her steamed two destroyers, *Wakeful* and *Grafton*, also laden with passengers.

To the crew of the lightly armed minesweeper, the destroyers' presence offered some assurance of protection. But the E-boats, armed with two torpedoes, two 20mm and one 37mm cannon, were fast and hard to spot. In mid-Channel, a tremendous detonation and a blinding flash of flame wakened the exhausted, sleeping soldiers huddled on deck, and shook the crew. It was *Grafton* that had been torpedoed.

Lydd was making towards the scene when there was a second explosion accompanied again by a searing eruption of fire, roiling smoke and the stench of burning oil. *Wakeful* had not quite lived up to her name. An E-boat had caught her napping too and she was going down fast.

In *Lydd*, the sounds of E-boats searching for more British vessels were all too clear. Her skipper decided that he would be doing the best he could for the greatest number of human lives if he made for the home shore than if he stayed in the hope of rescuing men from the water.

The minesweeper had not gone far when flames from a gun muzzle stabbed the darkness. Machine-gun bullets slammed into her and killed one of her crew.

A lookout called. The skipper, his passengers and the gun crews saw, against the faint glow from the two burning destroyers, the shape of an approaching small craft. It could only be an E-boat and the gunners opened fire. It wasn't. It was a British fishing boat, unhappily named *Comfort*, which had been picking up *Wakeful*'s survivors.

On a foggy night that same week, another fishing boat which, with its crew, had been taken over by the Navy and converted to minesweeping, was on its way to Dover, crammed with troops. In the almost impenetrable darkness and with not a glimmer of light showing from any vessel afloat in those waters, even a lookout posted right for'ard in the bows had no time to give warning of another craft. Nor could any vessel safely go at low speed: E-boats and the need to reach England, put the passengers ashore and return to France for another load made haste essential. The lookout did spot a boat ahead and shout to the bridge, but there was no time to change course. The trawler ran down a small boat in which Belgian troops had embarked in the hope of sanctuary in Britain.

These were sheer tragedies, but, as often happened with such accidents, there was farce soon after. It was enacted in one of the many trawlers converted from fishing to mine-sweeping. In those early months of war, especially after weapons of all kinds had to be abandoned in France, the Navy, Army and Air Force – for airfield defence – all suffered from a lack of guns. Trawler-minesweepers had low priority for defensive armament.

One of the weapons provided was the Holman projector. It seems incredible now that such an apparatus could be seriously intended as anti-aircraft armament. It consisted of a pipe similar to a mortar, of a bore wide enough to accept a hand grenade – which had a four-second delay fuse. The safety pin had to be drawn before inserting it in the barrel, which held the firing lever safely in place. At the bottom of the tube was an inlet for either compressed air or steam, the alternative propellants. Under air attack, the Holman's gunner would point the tube to a point in space where he thought the aeroplane might be in slightly over four seconds' time. He then opened a valve at the bottom of the tube, to let the propellant surge in, and watched the Mills bomb, re-sembling a quarter-scale pineapple, shoot out of the tube . . . and usually fall harmlessly into the sea without even having scared the attendant representatives of the Luftwaffe.

Taking into account the need to estimate the aircraft's height, its speed and the ship's, the wind speed and direction, the speed of the draught from bows to stern created by the ship's progress, the rocking and pitching motion at sea, was a task for a computer. This ludicrous ballistic conception was a waste of iron, explosive, and production and distribution time. At a phase of the war when materials were scanty and hours spent on labour precious, if it helped anybody other than those who made a profit from its manufacture, it could only have been the enemy.

Training in its use was given on board ship at a place where the projectile was fired harmlessly over a wall on to mud flats. The instructor, a rating of vast size, was reck-oned to have the most protuberant stern in the Service. There came a day when he must have rued the dimensions that Nature had bestowed on him. After several demonstra-tions, he neglected to check the pressure in the compressed air bottle before yet again shouting a warning 'Fire!' and pulling the lever that would send the air rushing into the tube.

The air supply had so diminished that it exerted enough pressure only to send the grenade slowly up the tube as far as its mouth. Then it fell on to the deck. The audience fled, but the instructor was too heavy to sprint, so he flung himself prone. It is said that it took three weeks to remove the grenade fragments from his buttocks and six months before he could sit down without pain.

Humorous episodes in wartime are a welcome rarity. In contrast, the daily reality of a combatant sailor's, airman's or soldier's life is found in an edict issued during 1940. It was an ordinance of particular callousness and cruelty, even in a year so shadowed by calamities and relieved only by the rescue of most of the British Expeditionary Force and the RAF's defeat of the Luftwaffe in the Battle of Britain.

It was the habit of some pilots to practise bomb-aiming by making dummy runs on ships at sea. Sometimes, in bad visibility, the RAF made real bombing runs on British vessels they had misidentified.

The Captain Minesweepers at a large north-east coast fishing port laid down that his ships must fire on every aircraft that approached, unless it were definitely identified as friendly. He offered a reward of £5 for every aeroplane shot down on patrol *and £10 if it belonged to the RAF.*

This criminal instruction ignored two relevant facts. One was that aircraft in distress – returning from a sortie with wounded men on board, fuel tanks holed, engine trouble – often deliberately alighted on the water near Royal Navy vessels, hoping for succour. The other was that air crews sometimes mistook the Oropesa floats, which minesweepers towed on half a mile of cable, for a U-boat's periscope and attacked it.

The senior officer who gave that order should have been court martialled and cashiered. If he had caused the death of even one RAF man, he deserved to be shot or hanged.

CHAPTER 6

By now it had become plain that it was essential to adopt
the resigned and practical attitude, hoping that some good
might come from the very bad, expressed in the mordantly
humorous verse of Harry Graham, so typical of macabre late
Victorian and Edwardian humour:-

<blockquote>
' "There's been an accident!" They said,
"Your servant's cut in half; he's dead!"
"Indeed!" said Mr Jones, "and please
Send me the half that's got my keys." '
</blockquote>

For RAF fighter pilots, the Battle for France and the Battle
of Britain in 1940 produced a special risk of death or injury
– that of mistaken identity by the civil population.

British pilots who baled out over France were likely to find
angry peasants with guns and pitchforks, who had assumed
they were German, awaiting their landing and sometimes
taking pot shots at them as they floated down. Civilians who
would have recognized the dark blue uniform of l'Armée
de l'Air and understood the French spoken by the man
who wore it had probably never seen an RAF or Luftwaffe
uniform or flying overalls; and a shouted *'Je suis anglais'*
in a foreign accent might not be comprehensible. Terror
and panic had spread throughout the country at the swift,
ruthless advance of the enemy in the wake of dive-bombers
and tanks. These did not hesitate to attack the refugees

who crowded the roads, which was not conducive to cool thinking by the natives anyway.

In England similar confusion existed. Although RAF uniforms were familiar to most people, few realized that pilots often wore white or dark blue overalls; and, again, people were jittery and apt to jump to the wrong conclusions. An added danger was the zeal of the Home Guard, ever on the lookout for the enemy – and all too frequently provided with a firearm. Regional dialects, in those days when radio had not made them as familiar as television now has, were another cause of misunderstanding: a Hampshire farmhand who had never heard a Geordie, Yorkshireman or Glaswegian could easily fail to understand a hasty 'I'm English', or 'British'. Worst placed for maltreatment were the Poles and Czechs who flew in RAF squadrons. Some spoke little English and those who could utter a few life-saving words did so in strange accents. The occasions when pilots were wounded or killed were concealed and have remained so. It is only personal narratives that reveal them.

Pilot Officer J. H. Lacey, DFM, came close to figuring in the relevant statistics on 13 September, 1940, when 501 Squadron had just moved to Kenley. A fifty-minute patrol had yielded nothing before the weather deteriorated. The pilots were relaxing in the crew room when the telephone rang and the duty controller in the Operations Room asked for a volunteer to take off and look for a Heinkel that was somewhere over London. 'But,' he warned, 'owing to the unbroken cloud over the whole of south-east England, whoever goes will probably be unable to land. It will mean baling out.'

'I've always wondered what it's like to bale out,' said Ginger Lacey, and scrambled.

It was a long stalk – he was airborne for two hours. The controller guided him eastward at 14,000 ft above the solid layer of cloud. A turn to the south, another to the east; a turn to the south-east, then east again. Until . . .

'I saw it slipping through the cloud tops, half in and half out of cloud, making for the coast. I didn't know where I was, because I hadn't seen the ground since taking off. I dived on him and got in one quick burst, which killed his rear gunner. I knew he was dead because I could see him lying over the edge of the rear cockpit. Of course the Heinkel dived into cloud and as I was coming up behind him I throttled hard back and dropped into formation on him, in cloud. He turned in cloud two or three times, still making a generally south-easterly direction and I'm quite certain he thought he had lost me or that I'd stayed above cloud. Actually, I was slightly below and to one side. You couldn't see very well in cloud, through the front windscreen of a Hurricane, but you could see through the side quarter-panel and I was staying just close enough to keep him in sight through this. I stayed with him in all his turns. He made one complete circle and then carried on south-easterly. Eventually he eased his way up to the top and broke cloud, presumably to see if the fighter was still hanging around. Just as he broke cloud and I was dropping back into a position where I could open fire, the dead gunner was pulled away from his guns and another member of the crew opened up on me, at a range of, literally, feet.

'I remember a gaping hole appearing in the bottom of the cockpit. The entire radiator had been shot away and I knew it was just a matter of time before the engine would seize, so I put my thumb on the firing button and kept it there until my guns stopped firing. By that time he had both his engines on fire and I was blazing quite merrily too. I think it was a glycol fire rather than an engine fire, but *what* was burning didn't particularly interest me: I knew that *I* was burning and I was going to have to get out.

'As soon as the guns ran out of ammunition, by which time the He111 was diving steeply through the cloud, I left the aircraft.

'I came out of the cloud in time to see my aircraft dive into the ground and explode. While drifting down, I saw various people running across the fields to where it had crashed. There was one man passing almost underneath me, when I was about five hundred feet up, so I shouted. This chap stopped and looked in all directions, so I shouted again.

"Right above you". He looked up and I saw that he was a Home Guard.

'As he saw me, he raised a double-barrelled shotgun to his shoulder and took aim. I knew it was a double-barrelled gun because I was looking down the barrels and they looked like twin railway tunnels!

'I shouted "For God's sake don't shoot" and amplified it with a lot of Anglo-Saxon words I happened to know, and continued to exhort him not to shoot for the rest of my way down; and added a lot more Anglo-Saxon words.

'Eventually I fell in a field and just sat there, but he still kept me covered with his gun. I said, "Hang on a minute while I get at my pocket and show you my identity card." He put his gun down and said, "I don't want to see your identity card – anyone who can swear like that couldn't possibly be German." '

This was Lacey's tenth confirmed victory and the Heinkel was the one that had just bombed Buckingham Palace.

A bale-out that did not end so happily and which encapsulated the dangers peculiar to RAF pilots whose command of English made them suspect, was witnessed at Wapping, in London's East End. This part of Dockland figured in a music hall joke about the revivalist preacher who welcomed his congregation with the words, 'I am delighted to find so many repentant sinners here . . . *Wapping* sinners.' There was nothing at all to smile about in the greeting offered to a baled-out Hurricane pilot during the time when London was being heavily bombed.

An enemy raid had been intercepted on its approach up the Thames Estuary. The Hurricanes and Spitfires forced the bombers to scatter and the fighting spread over the length of the river and on both sides. There came a moment when the men, women and children of Wapping saw a parachute open and drift down towards them.

There was loud speculation. 'One of our boys?' 'Might be a bloody Jerry.' 'Soon tell, when he lands.'

The feet of the man under the parachute touched the ground, he stumbled and fell. The air spilled out of the

71

canopy and he released himself from the harness, then stood up, dazed.

The watchers closed in. 'You all right, chum?' 'What's the matter with him?' Then, ' 'Ere, 'e's not wearing RAF wings! What's that on 'is chest, then?' Polish pilots in RAF uniforms wore their own Air Force's badge, a silver eagle; and, to signify that their country was in bondage to the Germans, its legs were fettered by a silver chain. 'Bleedin' Jerry, that's what 'e is . . . '

The pilot kept staggering and presently the people surrounding him realized that he could not see. There was no wound but he was, perhaps temporarily, blind. And then he spoke. He knew very little English, he was dazed, sightless, utterly confused.

He *must* be a German, jabbering all that gibberish. So they lynched him.

No 501 squadron had shifted to Colerne, near Bath, to re-equip with Spitfires, which had to be fetched from Exeter. Lacey ferried most of them and made sure that he was allotted the best as his personal aircraft. He and Wing Commander Beamish, who was the station's Wing Commander, Flying, had been up to practise dog-fighting. Coming in to land, Lacey noticed that the big, white-painted wooden 'T' outside the Flying Control tower, which showed wind direction, had been turned 180 degrees since they had taken off. He made his landing approach in the correct direction. Once he had touched down and let his tail drop, he could not see straight ahead, because the Spitfire's long nose was now upthrust at a sharp angle.

Half-way along the runway he was hurled forward in his straps with a violence that threatened to tear them apart. There was a deafening clang of rending metal, his windscreen and canopy shivered into a myriad cracks, his engine screamed and died. He heard the siren and bell of a fire engine and ambulance racing towards the crash.

Wing Commander, Flying, who had not spotted that the landing T had been reversed, collided with him head on.

Extraordinarily, neither was killed nor seriously injured. A friendly collision in all respects, but for the senior officer's injured pride.

It was not long after that when a real shooting 'blue on blue' occurred – with Ginger as the perpetrator. The squadron had been posted again, this time to Chilbolton, a satellite of Middle Wallop, in Hampshire. He had been promoted to Flight Lieutenant and given command of 'A' Flight. There was a new Squadron Commander, with fourteen confirmed kills, Squadron Leader A. H. Boyd, DFC (and bar), who had joined the Royal Navy as a cadet in 1926 and in 1933, as a sublieutenant, transferred to the RAF.

Every night the squadron flew patrols over Portsmouth. With three or four aircraft airborne at the same time, stepped at 2000-foot intervals, pilots were ordered to stick rigidly to their allotted levels. Lacey was at the top of the stack one night when he saw, against the glare of a fire in the docks and a searchlight beam, a Junkers 88. Here was the chance that everyone in the squadron had sought for seven months – to bring down its first hostile aircraft by night.

The bomber circled lazily, no doubt admiring the effects of its, and its companions', work. Cagily, Lacey brought his Spitfire round until he was a hundred feet above and to one side. With the target comfortably in his reflector sight, he triggered his guns. Bright flashes of the recently issued De Wilde ammunition flashed along the enemy's fuselage.

The Ju88 dived and he followed it. The strong light from below dazzled him and he lost his quarry. He found it again and touched off a short burst. It disappeared; presently it reappeared and he fired a third time. Two or three thousand feet slipped by while he kept losing it and finding it again, forgetful of the stricture about staying at his briefed height. When he finally managed to keep it in view without its evading him, its turns became tighter and faster until it was holding its own with the Spitfire. This baffled him.

In his headphones the mush of the radio carrier wave gave way to a voice. He heard his Commanding Officer, who was patrolling at the level immediately beneath his, inform the controller that he had been harassed by machine-gun fire and there was a fighter on his tail.

In Lacey's own words, 'A thought crossed my mind.'

He called the C.O.: 'Please flash your navigation lights.' As he had suspected, the aircraft he was trying so hard to shoot down blinked out a series of bright flashes.

The Ju88 had got away – with several bullet holes and perhaps dead or injured men aboard – and he had to lean heavily on Adrian Boyd's sense of humour when they met in the crew room an hour later.

For bomber crews, there was always the risk that poor aircraft identification by anti-aircraft gunners would be their doom. Those that had to cross the French coast twice, on their way to bomb targets in Germany and on their return trip, were often fired at. In March, 1940, a 149 Squadron Wellington on its way home had been shot down by a French coastal battery. Six months later, another of the squadron's Wellingtons, returning from a raid on Berlin, was so badly damaged by British anti-aircraft guns on the north side of the Thames Estuary that it had to make a forced landing in which it was irreparably damaged. By the end of the war in Europe, Wellington squadrons were to lose thirty-three aircrew killed and seven badly wounded in this way.

When Italy declared war on Britain and France in June, 1940, it did not make the British tremble. The general notion of the Italians was a stereotyped caricature: of opera singers, barbers, ice cream vendors, waiters and owners of small restaurants in Soho – all of them exhaling the smell of garlic. In the Great War they had been allies of Britain and France, but their military reputation was associated only with the Battle of Caporetto in 1917, when they retreated rapidly and over a great distance in the face of a massive Austro-German onslaught.

It was an unkind assessment, for the enemy had every advantage. Being a rational people, the defenders saw no sense in dying uselessly, so quit the field. Of the slower runners, 20,000 were taken prisoner. Nobody ever gave Italy the credit it deserved for the excellence and bravery of its air force in that war.

In 1940 the only threat that Italy posed to Britain was in North Africa. Egypt was a British protectorate and its neighbour, Libya, an Italian colony. On the ground 36,000 British, New Zealand and Indian troops faced an Italian and colonial force of 300,000. In the air 176 RAF aircraft opposed 282 Italian.

In the Western Desert it was, naturally, the British who took the initiative. The Italian Army and Air Force, characteristically, showed no enthusiasm for a fight. At first light on 11 June the RAF took off to bomb the major airfield at El Adem, near Tobruk. On the 14th the British Army moved into action, crossed the Libyan frontier and captured Fort Capuzzo, an important stronghold. Between then and mid–September the Italians had 3,500 casualties; the British, 150. On 13 September Marshal Graziani sent six divisions to move cautiously towards Egypt. They halted after fifty miles and set up a perimeter of fortified positions.

The 3rd (King's Own) Hussars arrived in Egypt in September, 1940, and joined the 7th Armoured Division in the desert. A nineteen-year-old second lieutenant who ended the war as a major with a DSO, MC and bar recalls 10 December, three days after General (later Field–Marshal Sir Archibald) Wavell had initiated another strong advance. It was evening when his squadron attacked Sidi Barrani from the west and quickly forced its way through four miles of intricate defences. He came to a position that was strongly defended by Breda machine guns, where 'Two bursts of Vickers produced a horde of shouting, pleading and gesticulating prisoners, hands aloft, waving white handkerchiefs'. He sent them off to the rear – a small part of the total bag of 40,000 prisoners taken during those few days.

Then suddenly, as it was getting dark, the white walls of the village that was their next objective appeared and 'a wave of infantry came running from the direction of the town. We could see the evening sun glistening on their bayonets as the

75

little black figures doubled towards us.' Enemy infantry that showed fight? In the twilight, so it seemed. 'We fired several bursts at them, fortunately without inflicting any casualties, before we realized that they were the Cameron Highlanders, who had entered the battle from the east.'

Not long after this he 'unintentionally hurt the feelings' of a 7th Hussars squadron leader – and nearly wounded that officer physically. There had been a brisk encounter with the enemy, who were now surrendering avidly, but some were so scared that they had to be routed out of their dugouts. He was 'so carried away by the excitement of it all' that he was shouting at 'the terrified prisoners in an endeavour to get them into some sort of order. I addressed a ragged figure in a torn greatcoat in somewhat abusive terms. When he failed to respond, I fired two pistol shots at his feet. My consternation was complete when he revealed himself to be a British major.'

A few nights later, a tank commanded by another young lieutenant opened fire on four vehicles that had failed to halt when ordered to do so. In the dark, the red crosses on their canopies did not show up. 'The squadron area was filled with the moans of the wounded.'

In February, 1941, deliveries of the Spitfire Mk V had begun. There was more than one variant, differently armed. The Mk VB, which instead of the usual eight machine guns had six plus two 20mm cannon, caused particular interest.

The Me109 was armed with cannon, as its pilots had amply demonstrated by their slaughter of thousands of children, women and old men who had crowded the roads of France, trying to get away from the battle zone. This was all part of the Blitzkrieg. *Les sales boches* were clearing the way for their tanks, and lorries loaded with infantry – both of which drove straight over the dead and wounded, the crippled and infirm, the old folk and children who could not run from them, left in their path. In Britain nobody had yet been able to analyse the effect of cannon fire when aircraft strafed ground forces. A demonstration was therefore arranged. Salisbury Plain was the obvious place. It being hardly practical to experiment on troops, a convoy of lorries was to be the target.

The high-ranking RAF and Army officers and some civilians who, because of their technical or political interest, were invited, were coralled in an enclosure at a safe distance from what, in battle, would be termed 'the killing ground'. The scene is readily pictured: an abundance of red gorget patches and gold-braided cap peaks; inter-service chatter with its usual sub-text of rivalry; the pipe and cigarette smoke, no doubt a silver flask of whisky or cognac raised here and there.

Six Spitfires came swooping into view with the sweet sound of Merlin engines, music to an airman's ears, to which a few seconds later was added the sound of gunfire and the explosions of shells. Five aeroplanes flailed the lorries, ripped their canvas tilts to ribbons, tore great holes in their bodywork and blasted the engines to fragments.

The sixth directed all its destructive power at the spectators. As the din of aero engines and gunfire diminished, the cries of injured and dying men arose. Two Generals and three other senior officers were killed, some twenty others wounded.

The photographs taken by a War Office photographer were confiscated, secrecy was enjoined on all who had witnessed the lunatic act. The perpetrator was variously rumoured to have been a Pole who went berserk or simply aimed badly; a traitor working for Germany; or an ordinary British squadron pilot who was already crazed by too much operational flying and driven completely mad at that moment by the noise and flames and general reminders of combat. In the archives where the proceedings of Courts of Inquiry, Summaries of Evidence and Courts Martial are held, the truth is presumably concealed.

Anyway, the five aircraft that did shoot up the legitimate objective provided enough evidence on which to base the statistics that had been sought about the effects of ground strafing on the human body as well as vehicles – quod erat demonstrandum.

The 3rd Hussars had fought in every major battle and countless smaller engagements since the tracks of their light tanks first bit into the desert sand. They had shared in the triumph of driving the Italians back in confusion right out of Cyrenaica, Libya's eastern province. It had not been an easy victory all the way. Roy Farran, DSO, MC and bar, who was then a subaltern in the Regiment, pays the Italians a respectful tribute. They had brought a new armoured division equipped with the M13 medium tanks to North Africa. This whole division was sent into action. Eight cruiser tanks of the 2nd Armoured Division were positioned 'around a pimple-shaped mound on which stood the mosque of Beda Fomm'. They broke wave after wave of the new enemy tanks, which were 'coming in along the line of the road in batches of thirty'. Each time, the cruisers stopped them. 'Their crews were brave enough, but their tactics were almost too crude to be sane . . . the battle went on all day, until the pimple by the mosque was littered with burning tanks.'

The way lay open to sweep on across Tripolitania, capture Tripoli, Libya's capital, and bring the entire Italian forces in North Africa to surrender.

The first Luftwaffe units had arrived in Libya in the first week of February, 1941. The German Army's advance guard landed on 14 February. This was the right moment at which to launch the final assault before the Germans, so much more formidable than the Italians, could enter the battle in strength.

The British, Australians, New Zealanders and Indians were now deprived of total victory in this theatre of war by one of the most disastrous decisions made by Winston Churchill and his War Cabinet. They ordered Wavell to halt the advance and transferred some of his best troops and several RAF squadrons to Greece to meet the invasion that the Italians and Germans had launched there.

Wavell's army fell back to Tobruk, which they had recently captured. The majority had to stay and endure a long siege. In the 3rd Hussars lots were drawn to decide whom they would be. One of those who were sent back to the Nile Delta by sea was a subaltern just twenty years old. It was May, and after a few days' leave his squadron was on its way to Crete, whither the defenders had withdrawn from the Greek mainland.

Immediately they were put ashore they were embroiled in the fighting. They saw the German paratroops land on 20 May. Abandoning their breakfast, they ran to mount their tanks. In a few minutes this youngster's tank was bowling along a road when the way was blocked by a barrier. A Schmeisser fired at it from the olive trees where paratroopers were hiding. The tank raked the trees, hoping to hit the enemy the crew could not see.

Then, a macabre scene: 'There occurred one of the tragedies of war which make it a bitter, evil business having nothing to do with God. I saw what appeared to be a German in a long grey overcoat coming up the road towards us. It was difficult to see through the visor and I had never seen a German at close range before, but it looked like the real thing to me.' He ordered the gunner to fire. Bullets struck the road around the grey-clad figure, but still it walked on. 'Suddenly I shouted to the gunner to cease fire. It was a woman, a civilian, and I had shot her. She came on and we could hear her screaming now. The Germans had stopped firing and there was nothing but her screams. She was an old peasant woman in a long grey dress, her grey hair done in a bun behind her neck, and she was holding out her hands for mercy as she screamed. Her shoulder had been shattered by a bullet, splashing her dress and her wrinkled face with blood. What had I done? I tried to stop her, but she went on up the road towards the village, staggering, screaming.'

The tank moved on until a Greek lying in a ditch waved a handkerchief and it stopped. The Greek put a finger to his lips and pointed with the other hand to a figure lying in the ditch on the other side of the road. It was a German parachutist. 'I levelled my heavy forty-five Smith and Wesson and said, "Come on, surrender, you Jerry bastard." The German did not move. I fired a round and he flinched as though I had hit him, but I was not to be foxed, because I had seen the dust kicked up by my bullet at least four yards away. I tried with four more rounds, each with the same result. At last, in desperation, I told the gunner to turn the Vickers on him. He did not flinch any more.'

Further along they killed two more paratroops in the same way. This brought five more out of the olive grove with their hands up, although the tank commander had not meant to fire in that direction. Now comes the 'too late, mate,' syndrome. 'I was not in any mood to be taken in by any German tricks and in any case the affair with the old Greek woman had made me too miserable to care. I ordered the gunner to fire. Three dropped dead, but two others managed to limp away. I do not think that I would make a practice of shooting prisoners, but Crete was different, and in the heat of the moment I had not time to think.'

It was to be a hat-trick of assorted variations on the literal theme of friendly fire. As the tank went on its way, a New Zealander shouted a warning that the enemy had taken the dressing station.

The young officer told his driver to go slowly. The dressing station was twenty yards away, brown marquees under the trees. Three Germans stood round two British trucks over which they had draped swastika flags. 'We bowled them over into the ditch with the first burst.' Among the tents stood others with guns trained on several medical orderlies seated on the ground with their hands on their heads. 'We fired a careful burst. The Germans scattered and I believe some of the New Zealanders managed to escape in the confusion.'

CHAPTER 7

Many a woman has found a husband by putting into practice the adage that 'the way to a man's heart is through his stomach'. Many a nation has lost a war because the stomachs of its population have been brought to starvation. In modern wars it is not food alone that is essential to sustain a country's armed forces, its industrial production and the health and morale of all: oil and raw materials are other essentials. The British public did not know at the time, nor have later generations realized, how close Britain came to having a famine diet forced on her and reduction of manufacturing output to a level that could not enable her to continue fighting.

The First World War had seen the growth of a German submarine fleet that preyed heavily on Britain's supply routes. Hitler's war had unleashed not only an even more destructive undersea fleet, but also long-range aircraft that could both report the movement of ships for the U-boats' information and sink them. The Atlantic Ocean was their main hunting ground and the Battle of the Atlantic, in which the opposing navies and air forces were in conflict from the first day, would ultimately decide Britain's survival or defeat. With the fall of France in June, 1940, Focke-Wulf Condors began operating from the airfield at Bordeaux and U-boats from France's Biscay naval bases. By the end of October the Condors, which could cruise 1100 miles out to sea, carried a 4600 lb bomb load and bristled with cannon and machine guns, sank over 90,000 tons of Allied shipping. In November, 1940, they accounted for eighteen ships totalling 66,000 tons. U-boats were even more destructive: in the same month they sank 63 ships amounting to 350,000 tons.

Germany's surface vessels posed a further threat to Allied convoys. By abrogating the Versailles Treaty, Hitler had built two fast new battleships and another, bigger and faster, was on the stocks. While watchers on the coasts of Europe, from Norway to Spain, informed British Intelligence in London about the movements of German warships, British agents in the German naval base at Kiel had been reporting progress in the building of the latest vessel, *Bismarck*. In May they sent word that her trials in the Baltic Sea had been completed. With her armament of eight fifteen-inch, twelve five-point-nine-inch and sixteen four-point-one-inch guns, she was the most formidable individual menace to British shipping: her biggest guns outranged the Royal Navy's. Add armour plating that was up to twelve inches thick, and she became an immensely difficult vessel to sink. Her size can be judged by the number of her crew – 2300. This single addition to the fleet of battle-ships and battle cruisers could double the monthly losses.

Bismarck sailed for the Atlantic on 19 May, 1941. The British knew where she must be bound; and the Germans knew they must know. The Commander-in-Chief Home Fleet sent the cruisers *Norfolk* and *Suffolk* to patrol the Denmark Strait, which lies between Iceland and Greenland. The Luftwaffe flew reconnaissance sorties over the same area.

On 21 May a photographic reconnaissance Spitfire based at Wick, in Scotland, made a flight over the Norwegian coast. It landed at 1300 hrs with photographs that showed a Hipper class cruiser and *Bismarck* in Grimstadt Fjord, south of Bergen.

There were four possible routes for *Bismarck* to take. A battleship, a battle cruiser, three cruisers, six destroyers and five armed trawlers of the Home Fleet put to sea to cover these. Between 2155 hrs and 2330 hrs eighteen Coastal Command aircraft took off to search. The following day Fleet Air Arm Albacores joined the hunt.

That afternoon the RAF found that the quarry had left the fjord. On this confirmation that she was definitely at sea, the rest of the Home Fleet sailed for the North Atlantic: making a total of five battleships, three battle cruisers, fourteen cruisers, twenty-two destroyers, two aircraft carriers, two submarines and five trawlers. Among them was the carrier *Victorious*, with six Fulmars and six Swordfish aboard. The scale of effort gives the measure of the threat posed by Germany's newest battleship to the eleven British convoys then in the waters for which she was heading.

There was a thick mist in the search area. At 1920 hrs on the 23rd *Suffolk* sighted *Bismarck* and the heavy cruiser *Prinz Eugen* at a range of eight miles. She hid in the mist and tracked the enemy ships on radar until they had passed, then emerged and followed them.

Norfolk, also hiding in the mist, showed herself an hour later, to see *Bismarck* five miles off and heading straight towards her. The German ship opened fire and her shells straddled the cruiser, which promptly hid again. Later that night *Bismarck* reversed her course and challenged *Norfolk* and *Suffolk*, which both also went about and were concealed in a squall that turned into a snow storm.

In this fashion the hunt continued. On the 24th three more battleships, three cruisers, nine destroyers and an aircraft carrier, *Ark Royal*, were diverted from convoys in the Azores and Gibraltar areas to look for *Bismarck*.

At 1500 hrs on the 24th a third carrier, *Victorious*, sailed from Scapa Flow. She was newly commissioned and her pilots had never done a deck landing. At 2210 hrs nine Swordfish and Fulmars took off into cloud and rain, with one hour and forty minutes ahead of them before darkness would fall. After an hour's search they saw a ship that they thought was the fox that they and the huge, heterogeneous and widespread pack of hounds were hunting. They were disappointed to find that she was *Norfolk*. A moment later they saw *Suffolk* near her. They flew on and presently *Victorious*'s radar gave an echo on to which *Victorious* homed her aircraft. This time the false alarm proved to be a U.S. Coastguard cutter. (America wasn't in the war yet, and wouldn't be for another seven months.) They turned away and there, six miles ahead, could see a ship that really was *Bismarck*. They broke formation at once and attacked with their torpedoes from several directions, while the enemy battleship put up a retaliatory barrage of flak. One of the torpedoes hit and there was a tremendous explosion in *Bismarck* amidships.

It was dark by now. The homing beacon aboard *Victorious* was unserviceable, so she switched on a searchlight, in defiance of lurking U-boats. Two Fulmars had been lost. In difficult circumstances the surviving aircraft landed.

By this time Coastal Command Hudsons, Catalinas and Sunderlands were in the hunt. There were various momentary contacts with *Bismarck*. Once, she broke wireless silence and her signal was picked up by the Admiralty. A Catalina flying boat, accidentally breaking cloud, spotted her and was instantly fired on. The aircraft, its hull damaged, had to abandon its patrol. Two Swordfish, flying separately from *Ark Royal*, reported sightings of what might have been either the heavy cruiser *Prinz Eugen* or *Bismarck*. It was indeed the elusive new battleship and in the continuing hide-and-seek two of *Ark Royal*'s aeroplanes shadowed her for hours.

All the circumstances of this urgent, anxiety-ridden pursuit, in which the weather was in the enemy's favour and the initiative in his hands, bred an atmosphere of tension that infused every active and vicarious participant. Parliament, the Admiralty, the Air Ministry, the crews of the ships and aircraft and, through the press and BBC, the public, were involved. It was a bedlam in which instant decisions had to be made in situations of uncertainty by men under extreme stress. For airmen, the problem was compounded by speed, poor visibility and atrocious weather.

The Swordfish that had taken off from *Ark Royal* had been told where *Bismarck* was estimated to be. They had also been told that there were no British vessels near her. They were plugging through the mist and rain when a warship appeared ahead and it could only be *Bismarck*. Their certainty was based on out-dated information: a signal informing their carrier that the cruiser *Sheffield* had been sent into the area had not been received until that moment.

Ark Royal's captain abandoned security and, in plain language, made a signal to his aeroplanes at once to warn them. He was not in time. The only fact that could give him any comfort was that *Sheffield* had acted as target for his Swordfish when they were making dummy attacks during training: the pilots should therefore recognize her, however unexpected an apparition she might be.

All the conditions, however, were against the application of cool judgement. The ship was rolling and pitching in heavy weather, the visibility was poor, her once well-known shape was obscured by wraiths of mist and the deep troughs, tall waves and wind-driven spume of a turbulent sea. The aircraft had burst upon her suddenly, with no time for their crews to register any familiar features. Attack was the only thought that filled their minds; and a good torpedo attack demanded total concentration on technique.

The cruiser's captain had kept the aircraft in view through his glasses as soon as the lookout reported them. He was expecting them to overfly his ship and was thunderstruck when they dived with the plain intention of launching their torpedoes at her.

With the helm hard over and at full speed, heeling like a racing dinghy, tall waves leaping on either side of her sharp bows, the wake boiling in the already tumbling sea, *Sheffield* turned tightly. Three . . . four . . . five . . . six explosions made the air tremble as torpedoes that had been dropped too steeply detonated on impact with the waves, while *Sheffield* changed course again and yet again, dodging between the tall fountains of spume and dense grey-green water that were flung up around her. Then, to the relief of everyone aboard, the pilots who had not yet attacked pulled away. They had seen the white ensign.

The ship's company was at action stations, but no fire order had been given. Discipline held. Not a shot was fired at the friendly attackers throughout those horrifying moments.

The frantic chase ended on 27 May. At 0847 hrs, two battle-ships, *King George V* and *Rodney*, and two cruisers, *Norfolk* and *Dorsetshire*, engaged *Bismarck*, which fought back.

Then Swordfish from *Ark Royal* appeared. They flew over *King George V* and asked for a cease fire so that they could make a torpedo run, but nobody could spare a moment to heed them.

One of *King George V*'s anti-aircraft crews, however, did give their attention to the aeroplanes: by loosing off at them – until they realized their mistake. They had missed, anyway.

At 1036 *Bismarck* went down.

The British convoys that took war materials to Russia had one of the war's most uncomfortable duties. The seas were rough and in winter there were ice floes. For many months of the year the cold was so intense that flying spray froze as soon as it touched any part of a ship or anyone aboard. The hardships were mocked by Stalin, who ordered that all signs of British or American origin must be removed from the tanks, motor vehicles and other cargo as soon as they landed. They were then replaced by 'Made in the USSR'. All dictatorships are founded and depend on lies and deceiving the people and this was a particularly shabby example.

In December, 1941, a convoy between Britain and Russia was attacked for the first time by German torpedo aircraft, which sank three merchantmen. Soon after, the Asdic sets in two destroyers, one British and the other Norwegian, picked up signals that indicated the presence of a submarine. The area had been declared free of British submarines, so both ships concluded that they had found a U–boat and dropped depth charges on it. They felt the usual shock waves thud against their hulls, heard the dull booms of explosions and saw the towering waterspouts that burst up from the sea. Slowly, the black bows of the submarine broke the sur-face. The destroyers opened fire. As the presumed U-boat began to sink, men appeared on her conning tower and decks, then tumbled dead or wounded. The Polish ensign broke out and the British ships stopped shooting. They launched lifeboats and picked up survivors. The Polish submarine was a hundred miles from where she was supposed to be.

It was a blighted end to a year when Britain's fortunes were at the nadir.

The RAF hated the Brest Peninsula. The town of Brest itself, at its western extremity, was one of the French Navy's biggest bases. Now in German hands, it had one of the strongest anti-aircraft defences in occupied Europe. A frequent target for bombs, it was attacked seven times in April, 1941, five times in May and raids went on monthly. From the local airfield Me109 and Me110 fighters operated. These were a particular scourge of Coastal Command Wellingtons based in Devon and Cornwall, which had to fly within their range when on the way to patrol the Bay of Biscay for U-boats.

St Nazaire, at the peninsula's south-east corner, near the mouth of the River Loire, was also an important naval station. It too was on Bomber Command's visiting list and defended by both flak and fighters in formidable strength. The enemy had built what they thought were impregnable submarine pens. To date, they certainly had proved bomb-proof.

To venture near St Nazaire by sea or air was one of the most unattractive undertakings that one could contemplate. The naval installations were considered as a target for a combined operations assault early in 1941, but turned down because shoal waters and broad mud flats were thought to make them unapproachable. Nevertheless, early in 1942 it was selected for a Commando raid. The reason was that, if the attack were made at the time of a spring tide, there was a good prospect of lightly laden craft being able to cross those mud flats. By now there was an added deterrent: the approaches were guarded by coastal artillery in abundance. This did not discourage the Planning Staff, who could offer at least the encouraging assurance that laying mines in the shallow water would be technically difficult; and an unlikely measure anyway, as the Germans would not think it feasible for assault vessels to cross there.

The raid's main purpose was to destroy the 35ft thick, 167ft by 54ft steel gate of the dry dock, which was 1148ft long and thus able to take any ship in the world. If the raid succeeded, *Tirpitz*, the biggest battleship afloat, would be unable to use it. Also, the submarine basin would then be tidal and no longer possible for U-boats to pass through at will on their way to the eight existing pens or the five more that were being built. Other targets were the gates' winding gear and the emptying pumps. An explosive device was to be fitted to the bows of HMS *Campbell* – formerly USS *Buchanan* – a destroyer, which was to ram the dock gate. Commandos were to land and attend to the demolition of the other objectives.

On 26 March, 1942, the raiding fleet sailed. In addition to *Campbell*, whose four perpendicular funnels had been replaced by two raked ones, to look something like a *Möwe* (Gull) Class enemy ship, it comprised two destroyers, sixteen motor launches, one motor torpedo boat and one motor gunboat.

That night the fleet hoisted German colours and changed course westwards. Next morning they attacked a U-boat. They did not sink it, but as the signal it made to St Nazaire said that they were on course towards the Atlantic, nobody suspected their true destination.

Fifty-five aircraft were to bomb the target, to distract the Germans' attention. Cloud level was 3000 ft. Owing to the risk of bombing the French population, only four of them did bomb, while the remainder stayed and orbited the town amid flak.

The ramming of the dock gate was scheduled for 0130 hrs on 28 March and the charge was expected to blow it up three and a half hours later. With the enemy colours replaced by battle ensigns, the assault went in. At 0115 hrs the attack alarm sounded ashore. Searchlights came on. Dazzled by the glare, the gunners aboard the small craft opened fire with their 20mm and 3-pounder guns, two-pounder pompom and

0.5-inch machine guns. The destroyers' big guns went into action. From the enemy came streams of tracer, machine-gun bullets, 20mm and 40mm shells.

There was a guard ship 400 yards offshore, directly in the path of the advancing fleet. Each ML fired at her in passing and one of the shore batteries, thinking she must be an enemy vessel, joined in so effectively that she sank.

Most of the MLs foundered or had to retreat, steering gear damaged and fuel set alight by tracer.

Campbell drove at the dock gate under heavy fire that killed two men on the bridge and others at her guns. Just before she rammed it, only four minutes later than planned, one of the RAF's big incendiary bombs crumped onto her foredeck, where the gun crew had already been killed or wounded. The Commandos stormed ashore from her and the MLs.

The survivors eventually made a fighting withdrawal across six miles of sea. *Campbell's* explosive charge went up at 1030 hrs. The raid cost the Commandos and Navy 169 lives and 200 men were taken prisoner.

This operation stands today as the war's most audacious and damaging act of sabotage.

In April, 1942, the 7th Motor Gunboat Flotilla was based at Lowestoft. On one of the many nights when the flotilla did anti-E-boat (German motor torpedo boat) patrols, MGB No 87, commanded by Lt S. B. Bennett, DSC, was in company with No 88, commanded by the senior officer, Lt J.B.R. Horne, DSC, and 89 with Lt C.D.W. Leaf in command.

Battles between small craft were particularly unpleasant because they had wooden hulls, which bullets and shells penetrated all too easily, and there was no shelter for gun crews on deck or anyone on the bridge. It was also a peculiarly tense form of warfare, groping about in the dark and knowing that if contact were made with the enemy the action would be sharp and furious, with little warning.

At about midnight 88 developed engine trouble, so her captain decided to hand over command to Bennett, in 87. This boat had no radar, so Bennett swapped boats with Leaf, who had been commanding 89, which did have radar.

For some reason, the two Lowestoft boats strayed into the patrol area of two MGBs from the Yarmouth Flotilla. The Yarmouth boats made the first sighting and challenged by switching on their recognition lights. No 89 responded – but, unfortunately, had hoisted the wrong lights. The Yarmouth boats therefore immediately opened fire. One had crept around astern of 89 and raked her with its two-pounder pom-pom, a heavy weapon indeed against a small inshore vessel. One burst killed both Bennett and the rating on the wheel. Meanwhile 87 had hoisted the correct lights and the attacker ceased fire.

This was the constant hazard of small craft operations and the closest analogy to night fighting in the air. A contact with the enemy demanded instant recognition followed by immediate action at rapid closing speeds.

A less depressing drama, more farce than tragedy, was enacted in a kinder sea a few months later. The stage was the Mediterranean, the backcloth the North African coast. A British minesweeper that had sailed from Algiers for Bône, 300 miles to the east, was some ten miles on her way and dusk was gathering, when a Heinkel 111 came upon her.

The captain's steward had, in peacetime, been a valet to rich or titled employers and now served his new master as assiduously as he had attended to the needs of peers and millionaires. The enemy air attack came in just as he arrived on the bridge ladder with a tray bearing the captain's customary evening mug of cocoa.

The growl of the low-flying bomber's engines, the explosion of bombs dropping into the sea and sending sheets of spray over the little vessel, the racket of the aeroplane's machine guns, and the minesweeper's modest armament prompted him to set the tray on deck and rush to a Lewis gun that nobody was manning. He lifted it from its mountings so that he could aim it at the Heinkel.

It had been raining. The deck was slippery. He skidded and his bullets sprayed the bridge – luckily without hitting anybody: except for one, which ricocheted into the captain's buttocks and perforated both cheeks on its way in and out.

The Heinkel got away unscathed.

Who would argue with St Paul when he enjoined on the Corinthians the platitudinous statement that 'All things are lawful for me, but all things are not expedient'? Certainly a certain private soldier of a distinguished line regiment would have found no fault in the morality of this dictum. Circumstances forced him to act in a manner that was both lawful and expedient.

One has only to put oneself in his shoes – ammunition boots, to be accurate – to justify his action on a night when he was on sentry duty while his battalion was still on home service.

In one of the empty barrack huts a miscreant had been locked up, to face a serious charge on the following morning. A huge, evil-tempered lance-corporal, renowned for his prowess on the rugger field and the readiness with which he resorted to violence, he had got drunk that night, taken exception to one of the subalterns and threatened to kill him. It was eleven o'clock and the sentry was perhaps nervous, uneasy about the responsibility of guarding so dangerous a prisoner. And midnight suggests its own horrors, as Milton knew quite as well as the young soldier.

'Hence, loathed melancholy,
Of Cerberus, and blackest Midnight born,
In Stygian cave forlorn,
'Mongst horrid shapes, and shrieks, and sighs unholy.'

'What shall I do if he breaks out?' the sentry asked his company sergeant major. 'Supposing he won't listen if I tell him to get back, and goes for me?'

The warrant officer's answer was short and uncompromising. 'Shoot him.'

The horrid shape of the drunken, murderous giant did break out and the sentry duly shot him.

The Colonel made no fuss about it. These matters are well regulated in the armed Services. The lance-corporal, probably lamented as a loss to the regimental XV, was buried; the private was posted to the Depot; the CSM was sent to another battalion.

CHAPTER 8

Three brief, perverse reminiscences of North Africa. The first is of a conversation that an RAF officer had with two American fighter pilots at the bar of an Allied Officers' club. It began with one of the Americans mentioning with amusement that a British light bomber had led him and his companion on a wild goose chase. 'We thought it was a Ju88, right? So we chase it half-way across the goddam Mediterranean before we catch up with it. Then we find it's one of yours – some airplane with a goddam Kraut kinda name.'

'A Blenheim, perhaps?'

'Yeah, that's right, a Blen-hyme.'

'So what did you do?'

'Why, we were so goddam mad we'd wasted our time, we both took a shot at it anyways.'

They missed – intentionally, they claimed.

The same officer had to spend a couple of days in an American transit camp. Soon after arriving he strolled from his tent to the nearest latrine, which bore a notice that it was for officers only. He was twenty yards away when he was stopped by a sentry.

'Speak English?'

'Of course. I *am* English.'

'Thought maybe you wuz Frahg. Them latrines is for ahfcers only.'

'I know. That's why I'm going there.'

The sentry unslung his rifle. 'Yeah? You an ahfcer?'

The flight lieutenant indicated the two strips of black and Air Force blue braid on the epaulettes of his khaki drill shirt. 'Don't you know an RAF officer when you see one?'

'Naw, I thought maybe you wuz some kinda corporal.'

The rifle was now at the high port.

'I'm a flight lieutenant – equivalent to your captain.'

'That right? You sure you ain't no corporal?'

'Want to see my identity card?'

'Yeah.'

After scrutinizing this, the sentry's gaze shifted to the Englishman's shorts and he grinned. 'Say, is them short pants reg'lar?'

The officer knew that 'regular' in the transatlantic distortion of English meant 'standard'. 'Yes. Haven't you seen newsreels and press photographs of British troops in the desert, these past few years?'

'Naw, I ain't never seen nothin' 'bout that.' But the private slung his rifle again and walked off – not bothering to salute.

The officer thought himself lucky that the sentry had not fired a warning shot before delaying him.

Group Captain Edwards-Jones – later knighted and an Air Marshal – was one of the most charming and courteous men in the Service. When commanding a fighter wing in Tunisia he had occasion to visit a nearby USAAF airfield, so drove himself there in his jeep.

The sentry at the gate stopped him, was not satisfied by his identity card nor impressed by the gold braid on his cap peak. As for the four strips of braid on each epaulette, to him they probably indicated 'some kinda master sergeant'. 'I got orders I gotta get permission from the Colonel afore I let anyone pass.'

There followed a telephone conversation between another sentry and somebody at, presumably, the camp headquarters. Several minutes passed.

The group captain had had enough. He put the jeep in

gear, his foot on the accelerator, released the clutch and drove through the gate.

He heard a rifle shot and felt a sharp pain in his foot. The sentry had fired at him and the bullet had not only ruined a perfectly good shoe and made a hole in the jeep's floor, it had also lopped off a toe.

In June, 1942, Rommel's Afrika Corps was driving the 8th Army, under the command of General Neil Ritchie, back over the ground that had been won under Wavell and Lieutenant-General Sir Richard O'Connor during the past two years. By 13 June the British had only twenty-five serviceable tanks left out of the 700 they had when Rommel opened his big offensive. The front line had already fallen back east of the Egyptian frontier. Tobruk had been abandoned and, after a sternly resisted siege, recaptured. Although the retreat was orderly, with no sense of panic, morale was in the balance.

Major Roy Farran, of the 3rd Hussars, was commanding a squadron which by now numbered only six tanks. To quote him: 'A long protracted retreat is even more tiring than a long advance. We were holding off the Germans with harassing columns and small patrols by day, while at night we would trundle back to new positions. This particular battle lasted six weeks from the time the Germans first attacked at Bir Hacheim. During this time we never had a proper night's rest.'

The Germans were hard on their heels and large numbers of Ju87s were dive-bombing their transport. The Afrika Corps had cut the British line in half by crossing a minefield 'as though it had never existed'.

Day and night the RAF bombed the enemy. Bostons were seen several times a day on their way to attack Rommel's vanguard. Morale was sustained by the sight of so much air activity. But . . .

'I remember one terrible night when there was supposed to be a hundred Wellington raid on German leaguers south of Matruh.'

The British were told to light fires in the shape of a

'V', pointing to the enemy line. The leading aircraft passed overhead and dropped their bombs on the target. Those that followed mistook the indicators for fires started by the first wave of Wellingtons and used them as markers for their own bombing. They dropped flares to illuminate the packed leaguer. Bomb doors opened. Five-hundred pounders came whistling down, to explode with deafening reverberations among men, tanks and lorries.

One of the RAF's most likeable characters was the late Group Captain R. W. 'Bobby' Oxspring, DFC, AFC, who joined the RAF before the war, fought in the Battle of Britain and ended the war with a score of twelve victories. In November, 1942, when commanding No 72 Squadron (Spitfires) in Tunisia, he was one of the many British pilots whose life was put in danger by inexperienced fighter pilots of the USAAF.

He described, with impeccable restraint and diplomacy, an operation of 18 December that year. 'We flew area cover for two American bomber formations. Twenty-four Bostons and an equal number of B17 Fortresses escorted by [USAAF] P38 Lightnings attacked the German-held port at Bizerta and the airfield complex at Mateur. Not surprisingly, the Luftwaffe reacted in strength to this lethal penetration of their air space and battle was joined in a big way. Initially we had some trouble with the Lightning escort whose pilots of the twin-engined, twin-tailed P38s were experiencing their first war combats. Their aircraft recognition was suspect and in surmounting this deficiency they just assumed that *any* single-tailed fighter was hostile. Anxious to blood themselves, they homed in on friendly and enemy fighters alike, and we spent some anxious moments dodging their headlong attacks.'

Despite such pests, there were blessedly fewer instances of blue on blue during the North African campaign than in the Great War and in other theatres of the Second World War. At the Second Battle of Alamein, which began at 2200 hrs on 23 October, 1942, part of the tremendous artillery barrage that accompanied the infantry and tank assault fell on the 51st Highland Division: a repetition of the most familiar form of self-inflicted damage since the invention of gunpowder. From now on it would be own anti-aircraft guns against aircraft and own bombs against ground forces that would be the most frequent and destructive cause of self-inflicted casualties.

Investigation has led to the conclusion that fear is the root cause of blunders when air operations miscarry because of mistakes made on the ground. Ever since 1916, when ground-strafing by aeroplanes was first practised widely, the first purpose-designed ground-attack aircraft were built, and bombing also became strategically and tactically predominant, aerial attack has held a special horror for soldiers.

Low-level strafing was always hated and feared. The words of a German officer in 1916 convey very well what it was like to have to endure this type of assault. 'The infantry had no confidence in their ability to shoot these machines down if they were determined to press home their attacks. As a result they were seized by a fear amounting almost to panic; a fear that was fostered by the incessant activity and hostility of enemy aeroplanes.'

An unfinished letter found on the body of a German soldier in 1916 read: 'We are in reserve but cannot remain long on account of hostile aircraft . . . the English are always flying over our lines . . . this moral defeat has a bad effect on us all.'

The effect carried over to 1939. Often, at the mere sound or sight of aeroplanes approaching, anti-aircraft batteries went to action stations and ships' gun crews closed up. Aircraft identification by those on the ground or at sea has always been weak. Sometimes gunners behaved with sheer idiocy. A Royal Canadian Air Force bomber pilot operating in RAF Bomber Command recalls of 1943: 'The jittery Army gunners always cut loose at you, despite the fact that we were flying north to south [en route from England to Germany] and there were eight hundred of us. We could hardly be Germans to the most unimaginative mind, yet they always pounded up the flak [he meant British A-A fire].'

The inference from all the evidence is that ground troops and sailors, in doubt whether the aero engines they could hear approaching heralded friends passing harmlessly overhead or foes about to unload thousands of pounds of high explosives on them, had a tendency to loose off just to be on the safe side.

There is another undeniable accusation of ungovernable alarm leading to hasty action: the equal and opposite reaction to intense flak of some timid bomber crews, who dropped their bombs prematurely and hurried away from a target at which they had not bothered to aim. This was much rarer than being shot at by excitable soldiers and sailors, as was proved by the flash-lit photographs that accompanied bomb release, but it was known to happen.

In November, 1942, British paratroops were dropped on Souk el Arba, in Tunisia. It was an occasion on which the RAF's meteorologists could have made a useful observation that would have saved many lives. Nobody had the prescience to draw the planners' attention to the fact that, in this part of the world, the air was more rarified than in Britain. This meant that parachute jumps could not be made safely from the same height as had been done during training at home. In consequence many men were killed or badly injured and containers damaged.

On the night of 9 July, 1943, when the invasion of Sicily began, units of the British 1st and United States 82nd Airborne Divisions, carried in aeroplanes and towed gliders, led the attack. A strong wind blew throughout the operation, from take-off in Tunisia to arrival in the battle zone, which made navigation difficult. Anti-aircraft gunners, both ashore and afloat, were warned to expect them, but lost their heads and put up a tremendous barrage. Out of 144 gliders, sixty-nine landed in the sea, some driven there by the wind, others released prematurely by confused pilots irresolute under fire. The Horsas floated, the Wacos broke up. Most of the gliders that did reach the shore were badly damaged by stone walls and anti-tank obstacles. The American paratroops were spread fifty miles along the coast, the British glider-borne troops were also much dispersed. Only twelve gliders were able to put down in the dropping zone. Among the 600-plus men killed and injured, 326 were drowned.

It had been intended that, on invasion night, the 1st Airborne Division would mount three operations ahead of the 8th Army, to accelerate its advance from the beachhead to cut off the German divisions in the centre of the island from the Straits of Messina. The target for each operation was a bridge.

The 1st Parachute Brigade's was the Primosole Bridge, six miles south of Catania, across the Simeto River, six miles south of Catania. It was guarded by barbed wire, fortified farm houses, road blocks and two pillboxes at each end. The River Simeto flowed north-west to south-east with many bends and passed under the bridge at a stretch that was both wide and tidal. Five hundred yards upstream it was joined by the River Gornalunga. The whole area was strongly defended, not least Catania airfield, and there were many dykes and ditches.

Seventy bombers would attack the airfield before the paratroops dropped, which should not only take out some of the flak but also start fires that would give the attackers helpful illumination.

At about 1800 hrs on 9 July the Brigade saw RAF Albemarle twin-engine reconnaissance bombers towing Horsa gliders and USAAF DC3 Dakotas towing Wacos fly over their camp, the gliders bucketing about in the near-gale. The Brigade's assault was postponed.

At 2245 hrs on 11 July an American force over 2000 strong, comprising men from a Parachute Infantry Regiment, a Parachute Field Artillery Battalion and an Airborne Engineer Battalion, was to be dropped near Gela, on the south-west coast of Sicily, by 144 aeroplanes of the US 52nd Troop Carrier Wing. The Army and Navy formations and ships in the area had been warned. In fine weather, the aircraft made landfall and flew along a two-mile-wide corridor across Allied territory at 1000 ft. The troops in the first wave jumped five minutes earlier than scheduled. The second wave was nearing the Dropping Zone when a machine gun opened fire on it. Immediately, all the Allied anti-aircraft batteries ashore and their naval counterparts began to shoot at the lumbering big troop-carriers. Tanks opened up on them with their heavy machine guns. Some paratroopers jumped, all were scattered widely, many were shot while descending or after touching ground.

The paratroops lost eighty-one killed, 132 wounded and sixteen missing. The air crews suffered seven deaths, thirty were wounded and fifty-three went missing. Twenty-three aeroplanes were destroyed and fifty-seven badly damaged. The inquiry that followed did not yield a positive verdict. The main cause of the amicide was attributed to inadequate training and poor discipline of Army and naval anti-aircraft gunners. Some units and ships denied having received notice of the operation.

The British 1st Airborne Brigade's jump was postponed to the 13th. They were carried in USAAF DC3s, in elements of three, of which only the leader had a navigator. The wing aircraft therefore had to remain in touch with it, whatever the weather or enemy action.

A paratroop officer who took part described the approach to the target. The aeroplane crossed the coast at twenty feet with quick-firing quadruple 20mm Flakvierling and louder 37mm sending up 'fountains of red and orange tracer'. The searchlights found the DC3, but it evaded them as tracer still flickered past. Two 88mm shells exploded close by and blew out the windows. With great skill the pilot zoomed and twisted over and around obstacles, then climbed steeply to five hundred feet. The green light came on and the shaken paratroopers jumped.

They found that they were alone on the dropping zone. Only one aircraft had followed them. 'The DZ should now have been filled with a swarm of men, but except for the odd dozen whom we had just seen, the plain was empty and apparently quite deserted.'

Then some Albemarles and Horsas came in. Some of the gliders caught fire, some crashed, some landed safely. The bridge was taken and held in more than twenty-four hours of heavy fighting.

The poor performance and fatalities on the first night had made the loss of life on the Primosole operation far greater than it need have been; or would have been if so many had not lost their courage at the crucial moment.

At about the same time, on the other side of the world, a US Marine Corps transport ship was sent to the bottom of the Pacific. The general impression was that a Japanese submarine had done it. In truth, it was (not the butler, but . . .) a US Navy patrol torpedo boat.

Meanwhile, RAF and United States Army Air Force squadrons in North Africa had been bombing military targets in Sardinia, in preparation for the landings in Sicily and Italy. The prime target was the port of Cagliari, the island's capital. The Sardinians, who, like most mainland Italians, felt friendly to the Allies, soon found that the American air crews' definition of 'military' was at variance with theirs. In accordance with the USAAF's and US Army's practice of saturating an area with fire in order to ensure that there was a substantial chance of hitting the target, they were more than a trifle inaccurate when releasing their bombs. This despite the boast that, with the Sperry bombsight, a bombardier (bomb aimer) could hit a pinhead from 15,000 ft. The pinheads, actually, were aboard the B17s, B24s et al.

On 12 April, 1943, la Marchesa Origo, who lived in southern Tuscany, noted in her diary: 'The American air raids on Cagliari – totally undefended after the first two attacks – have been entirely different from any executed by the RAF. The long queues of women and children waiting in the main street to enter the few shelters were repeatedly machine-gunned; the dead are over six thousand; and the few survivors have now taken refuge permanently in the caves round the town. A further horror is added by the fact that, during the first air raid, the terrified lepers escaped from their hospital and have now mingled with the rest of the population.

'When the first raids began, the following gentle prayer was said by the Sardinians:-

'*Ave Maria, grazia plena*
Fa' che non suoni la sirena
Fa' che non vengano gli aeroplani
Fa' che si dormi fino a domani.
Se qualche bombe cade giu
Madre pietosa, pensaci tu.
Gesù, Giuseppe, Maria
Fate che gli inglesi perdano la via.
Dolce cuore del mio Gesù
Fa' che gli inglesi non vengono più.'

Translated, this reads:-

Hail Mary, full of Grace,
Don't let the sirens sound,
Don't let the aeroplanes come,
Ensure that we sleep until tomorrow.
If any bombs do fall below
Compassionate mother, think of us.
Jesus, Joseph, Mary,
Make the English lose their way,
Sweet heart of my Jesus
Don't let the English come any more.

The diarist adds, 'A less bitter war prayer can hardly be imagined. But now, after the machine-gunning and whole-sale destruction [by the USAAF], the tone has changed and much bitterness is felt. In Naples, too, recent air raids have not confined themselves to "military objectives".'

Evidently some RAF bombs had also drifted off course, but the Italian lady makes it clear that the civilians whom they killed or injured were an insignificant number in comparison with those who felt the weight of Yankee bombardment.

Immediately upon their conquest of Belgium in May, 1940,

the Germans had taken over and enlarged the Minerva car factory at Deurne, near Antwerp airport. This make of car, with its trademark and radiator symbol of the helmeted head of the Goddess of War, was quite well known in Britain. In status it was equivalent in its own country to Rolls Royce there and Cadillac in America.

The factory now went over to the repair and servicing of damaged Luftwaffe aircraft and the installation in them of the latest modifications. Within three years 3000 people were employed in the plant itself and 400 on the airfield.

Belgian agents had kept British Intelligence informed of developments at the factory and, in March, 1943, sent a plan of its layout. Destruction of, or at least severe damage to, the factory was immediately decided upon. The attack was to be made by daylight on 5 April, 1943, by the US 8th Air Force, escorted by RAF Spitfires.

The day dawned fine, with thin cloud at 30,000 ft and clear visibility. Two diversions were flown, to confuse the enemy about the true target. One comprised twenty-five Liberators escorted by twenty-four RAF Spitfires. The second consisted of seventy-nine Flying Fortresses and twenty-four RAF Spitfires. After completing their feints they were to join up and accompany the main force of seventy-nine Fortresses, twenty-five Liberators and sixty RAF Spitfires.

No enemy fighters were seen during the spoof phase of the attack, but Me109s and FW190s were positioning themselves to intercept the raid. Eventually they shot down only four Fortresses. The Antwerp air raid sirens sounded at 1500 hrs and the flak defences reported that the raid was in sight at 1534 hrs.

The bombing that followed wrought carnage among the population, destroyed 220 private dwellings and damaged 3745 others. Among the 936 killed were 209 children in three schools, and 1342 people were injured.

Few bombs fell on the target and so little damage was done that the factory was in full production again within a few weeks.

★   ★   ★

Flying instructors at RAF operational training units and gunnery schools were vulnerable to a particularly irritating form of internecine assault. One of those who experienced it was probably the RAF's most unconventional and altogether bizarre character, George Frederick 'Screwball' Beurling.

To become a pilot at all and to join the Royal Air Force entailed a considerable struggle by him. It called for immense determination and many other good qualities, but also made him, understandably, even more bloody-minded than he was by nature. He was born in Canada, his father Swedish and his mother English. From boyhood determined to fly, he had great difficulty in obtaining and saving the money for flying lessons. When he qualified as a pilot he was too young for a commercial licence, so tried to join the Royal Canadian Air Force. Rejected because he did not meet the educational standard, he went to the United States to volunteer for the Chinese Air Force, in which there was an American fighter squadron, the Flying Tigers. Arrested for crossing the frontier illegally, he was deported to Canada. He applied to the Finnish Air Force, but his parents thwarted him by refusing to give their consent, which, as a minor, he needed: so he worked his passage in a cargo vessel across the Atlantic, jumped ship when he arrived in Britain and joined the RAF.

He was a wild youth, scruffy and rude, whom Service discipline irked. When, in early 1942, he arrived at an operational training unit, he had the good fortune to be instructed by Ginger Lacey who had his own ideas on discipline and had been heard to say, 'It's always the best pilots who get into trouble'. Of this pupil he said, 'There are no two ways about it, he was a wonderful pilot and an even better shot.' Beurling proved it by amassing a total of 31½ confirmed kills and winning the DSO, DFC, DFM and bar.

He earned fame when stationed at Malta, where he was the top-scoring pilot of the whole siege; and his nickname because he referred to the flies that infested the place as 'Goddam screwballs'. Group Captain Johnny Shaw, DSO, DFC, of the Royal Australian Air Force, who flew with him has recounted how he used to nominate his shots before going into an attack. 'Guess I'll get him in the starboard engine,' and sure enough, the enemy bomber's starboard engine would stop or catch fire. 'I'll shoot this guy in the cockpit,' and so it would be. 'I'll shoot his tail off,' and he would.

When Shaw returned to England in 1943 he was posted as a flight commander to the Central Gunnery School, where Beurling joined his flight as an instructor. 'He used to sit outside the rest hut with a two-two rifle and watch the birds flying past. A sparrow or starling would come by, he'd say how much deflection he was going to allow, then shoot it down.'

The local squire, an honorary member of the Officers' Mess, hearing that this much publicized character was on the station, invited him to shoot over his estate whenever he felt like it. Beurling, it seems, acknowledged the kindness with no more than a grunt. But one morning he did slouch off with a twelve bore to take advantage of it.

'The next day,' said Johnny Shaw, 'the squire turned up at the Station Commander's office in a fury, to complain. "That bloody man Beurling," he said. "He was in my woods yesterday and now there's not a thing moving . . . he shot everything that moved – including my gamekeeper [who, it transpired, took a charge of shot in the backside]." ' Beurling was unimpressed when the Station Commander passed on the complaint with a word of rebuke.

What happened shortly afterwards must have cheered the Squire no end. Beurling was engaged in an air fighting exercise with a pupil, the guns of both their Spitfires supposedly unloaded. Buerling's were, but it turned out that the pupil's was not. Having got his instructor in his sights, the pupil pressed his firing button for what should have been a camera gun photograph alone. A burst of bullets accompanied the photograph and Beurling's aeroplane caught fire. He baled out, pulled his ripcord too soon and his parachute did not open until he was dangerously near the ground.

Contemptuous of discipline anyway, he was also a good fellow at heart. Perhaps, too, he was lenient because his pupil had made so accurate a shot. He reported that his fuel tank had sprung a leak – not unusual when penetrated by a hail of .303 – and his explanation was accepted.

When the thousand-bomber raids began on the night of 30/31 May, 1942, they introduced a new danger for bomber crews. Thenceforward it was commonplace for hundreds of bombers to attack the same targets. Not all flew at the same height. The Halifaxes, Stirlings and Wellingtons flew lower than the Lancasters because of the disparities in their performance and other factors. These circumstances meant that, in addition to collision risk, aircraft were often hit by bombs dropped by others flying above them. By 1943 this became a major hazard. Sometimes they were incendiaries, which made loud and startling noises but did not detonate. Too often they were high explosives and demolished the aeroplane that they struck. Sometimes they pierced a hole through the top of the fuselage, another at the bottom and dropped right through without exploding. On occasion it was known for one to smash its way into an aircraft, but, instead of making another hole and falling through it, to remain inside, rolling and sliding about as the aircraft rocked and pitched, likely to blow up at any second.

The other great extra risk that entered the lives of bomber crews with these massive raids was that air gunners, their nerves stretched taut with the expectation of attack by night fighters, often mistook a friendly bomber for a Me110 or Ju87. It was all very well for Staff officers, and aircrew who were not air gunners – particularly not rear gunners, who had the loneliest job of all – to criticize them for mistaking a four-engine aeroplane for a two-engine type. But the majority of air gunners were aged between eighteen and twenty, few of them lived to fly enough operations to learn by experience, their task was enough to scare the daylights out of anybody who was not totally devoid of imagination, and aircraft identification in darkness and drifting cloud was like a game of blind man's buff. Criticism was not in the best of taste.

Despite natural empathy with the air gunners, sympathy must lie with the victims. When an air gunner in a Lancaster fired at a Stirling one night, he shattered its windscreen and hit the pilot, Sergeant Aarons, in the face, blinded him in one eye and wounded him in the chest and shoulders. Despite his serious injuries, Aarons kept his aircraft under control and dodged away; but he did not realize that he was still astern of his attacker. A second burst of shots wounded him again and he fainted. Members of his crew carried him to the rest bunk and gave him morphine, and one of them managed to fly the Stirling back towards base. Before they reached there, the pilot recovered consciousness, insisted on being carried back to his seat, landed the aeroplane and fainted again. He died soon after, but was awarded the Victoria Cross.

When the Allies invaded Italy in 1943 the main landing was made at Salerno on 3 September. One of the others was twenty-four miles south-east. This was the site of a Greek colony, Poseidonia, founded about 600 BC. In 273 BC it became the Roman colony of Paestum. The ruins of the Temple of Neptune, built circa 420 BC, are still standing.

A Field Security section of the British Intelligence Corps was attached to the Headquarters of the American Fifth Army that went ashore there on the late evening of 9 September. This handful of Britons was at once embroiled in a ferment of disorder engendered by the terror of raw troops badly commanded by raw officers. The next morning a FW190 strafed the landing area and dropped a bomb. Its reappearance every hour caused a hysterical reaction: soldiers kept leaping from concealment to point their rifles at anyone who caught their eye and bellowing a demand for a password – of which nobody had troubled to inform the Field Security men.

A couple of days later Fifth Army HQ was established a few miles away but still out of direct contact with any fighting. On 12 September the local American anti-aircraft gunners shot down their third Spitfire, which had just taken off to attack a FW190 and was at a height of only 300 ft. The sound of battle raged day and night, warships bombarded the enemy and German tanks were by now little more than a mile away.

On 14 September the Field Security unit and the rest of Fifth Army HQ were in an olive grove. The artillery and naval barrage intensified, the enemy tanks rumbled closer. The distraught American troops completely lost control of themselves. Imagining that German infantry had infiltrated their midst, they began shooting recklessly. As there were no Germans present, they were killing and wounding one another. The small British unit cleared off on their motor cycles, dodging the bullets the demoralized rabble were spraying around them.

CHAPTER 9

Simultaneously with the landings at Salerno, the British 1st Airborne Division had landed at Taranto. There was an anti-climax when, on the way from Tunisia by sea in British and American warships, a radio news bulletin announced the surrender of Italy. Instead of a strong defence of this valuable port, the Italians welcomed them as allies. A party from the Special Air Service, aboard a US Navy cruiser, was the first to go ashore – dramatically, down the mooring ropes as soon as the ship was made fast to a quay. It was dark when the last squadron disembarked with its jeeps, which were armed with twin Vickers aircraft-type machine guns. One squadron, commanded by a young, twice-decorated major, was ordered to push inland as far as possible up the main road.

They suspected that there might be Germans somewhere in the area, but it was impossible to guess where or how many. The Major positioned his ten jeeps on the left and right sides of the road alternately, his second-in-command leading and he himself in the second position. They drove slowly, stopping often to listen for sounds of other armed men on the move. The best reconnaissance by daylight is with the eyes, in darkness with the ears. After a few miles, the leader stopped and beckoned his CO forward.

The Major recalls: 'A number of armed figures were standing around a bridge a few yards ahead. As we peered into the half-light, an Italian sentry shouted a challenge. I called back that we were 'Inglesi' and began to walk towards them, telling my gunner to cover me with his Bren. I had just reached the bridge, on which stood a group of excited little men in green uniform, when a sentry rushed towards me with a brandished rifle and fired a round through my legs. The gunner filled him with a whole magazine of Bren bullets. And then there were profound apologies on both sides when we had established our identity. An officer produced a bottle of wine from which he insisted we drank a toast to our new alliance. Ignored by his friends, the dead sentry lay crumpled in the dust – an innocent victim of an accident of war. Before we moved on the officer gave me his address in Rome, but all his hospitality could not make us forget the body of a dead Neapolitan, lying unmourned on the bridge with his life blood running in the gutter, killed after the armistice.'

As the war progressed, the incidence of blunders became more frequent. Manifestly, this was a field in which few learnt from experience; except for the lesson that they had better keep as sharp an eye on their friends as on their enemies.

The last eighteen months of the war saw the worst: errors of judgment caused by idiocy, incompetence or total loss of self-control; as well as pardonable accidents that resulted from a breakdown in communication caused by enemy action.

The first month of 1944 found the RAF and USAAF enjoying such air superiority in Italy that they seldom had contact with the Luftwaffe. When flying behind the German lines, they found the roads almost totally deserted by day. Any vehicles that were on them stopped on sight of Allied aircraft, hoping not to draw attention, or made for the nearest place that offered concealment. RAF Intelligence had established that the longest time an enemy vehicle could be on any road north of the front line without being attacked from the air was five minutes. The German airfields were few and lay far behind the enemy lines. In contrast, the roads behind the Allied lines were always busy, the airfields were close to the Front and packed with aeroplanes. Only a fool flying over Italy could fail to know which side of the Front he was on.

Some American squadrons had evidently not registered the obvious differences between the two areas; nor had they learned to identify even the most frequently seen British aircraft.

One afternoon six USAAF Warhawk pilots were sculling around looking for something to shoot at. They spotted Trigno airfield, from which No 239 Wing RAF was operating. Evidently they did not even know whereabouts, geographically, they were; and the Wing's Spitfires might just as well have been Me109s or FW190s – even, so crass were these 'combat aviators', two- or four-engine bombers. They swooped in and strafed all too effectively, inflicting casualties on the fitters, riggers, armourers, electricians, radio mechanics and others who were servicing the aircraft. Their bullets lashed the storemen and clerks and MT drivers, the cooks and batmen and radio operators. They destroyed and damaged many Spitfires.

The whole disgraceful performance was witnessed by senior officers on another RAF airfield nearby.

No 239 Wing was commanded by the formidable Lieutenant-Colonel Lawrie Wilmot of the South African Air Force, whose excoriating comments to the perpetrators' Commanding Officer kept him at bay for several days. When the USAAF colonel commanding the field where the Warhawks were based felt that Wilmot's wrath had cooled to a safe degree, he flew in to apologize.

When he emerged from the interview and went to his aeroplane he found that, on the fuselage where it was customary to paint a swastika or iron cross for each enemy aircraft shot down, there were several RAF roundels to remind him of the Spitfires his irresponsible subordinates had written off. It was a characteristic touch of RAF humour and style, a silent but stinging rebuke.

The name Monte Cassino illuminates the pages of history. It is illustrious as the 1700-foot Apennine mountain-top on which, in 529AD, St Benedict established a monastery as the headquarters of the Order he founded, the Benedictines. In the annals of warfare it stands for unsurpassed heroism and determination on the part of both the defenders and attackers of what proved to be an almost insurmountable obstacle. To the Allied ground forces assaulting it, and to civilian inhabitants within some miles of it, its name is associated with monumental bombing errors.

From the invasion of Italy on 3 September, 1943, it took the Allies only until 1 October to capture Naples. To fight their way to the outskirts of Cassino town, which stood at the foot of the mountain, about half-way between Naples and Rome, took them until mid-January, 1944. In December, 1943, the Germans forcibly evacuated the town's 25,000 inhabitants. They had established their front, the Gustav Line, from the mouth of the River Garigliano on the west coast to the Rapido on the east. Monte Cassino was its pivotal point. The mountain's main asset was that, from its summit, observation could be kept over a great area. Also, if the monastery were used as a fortress, it was so strongly built that it would withstand a tremendous amount of battering: its walls were ten feet thick at the base and its longest side measured two hundred and twenty yards.

American, British, New Zealand, Indian, Polish and French Divisions of the Fifth Army took part in the assaults on it. The Battles of Cassino began on the night of 17 January, 1944, and ended on 25 May.

The first battle lasted three weeks and both sides had heavy casualties. The second battle saw one of those situations in which infantry advancing are so close to the enemy that shells fired in their support strike some of them down as well as the foe. It was the Royal Sussex who were victims: they endured five hours of shelling by both German and British guns. In the scale of casualties in this and the first and third battles it passed with little notice, overshadowed by a futile and chaotic operation that immediately followed it.

The original plan for launching the attack had been to coordinate a fighter-bomber strike with the ground assault. On 12 January Lieutenant-General Sir Bernard Freyberg, VC, Commander of the New Zealand Corps, was told that the USAAF had refused his request for air support. Late that night this decision was reversed and the air strike was confirmed for the next day. Meanwhile, after reconnaissance and discussions between Freyberg and the British and American Generals involved, plans were changed again and on the 13th morning the air operation was cancelled. Thenceforth, consultations between General Clark, who commanded the Fifth Army, Freyberg, Brigadier Dimoline, acting Commander 4th Indian Division, and others, led to further procrastination. The air attack was reintroduced, but as a mission for heavy bombers. Its date was changed from the 14th to the 15th. The main infantry attack would go in on the night of the 16th/17th. The air operation was timed for 1300 hrs, but the weather forecast caused the USAAF to bring it forward to 0930 hrs – a decision that was not passed to the New Zealand Corps until 0730 hrs.

Punctually at the new time, 135 B17 Fortresses bombed from between 15,000 and 18,000 ft. Only ten per cent of their bombs were on target. Forty-three B25 Mitchells and B26 Marauders, intrepidly dumping their loads from 10,000 ft, managed to do better: they brought down the west wall. Some units were not given warning of the attack. The British 7th Brigade had a few minutes' notice and took twenty-four casualties in consequence.

During the fighting on the ground, three British divisions lost over 4000 men; two American divisions lost 4200; some of the German companies lost three-quarters of their strength.

The record of the 34th United States Division is acknowledged to rank with the finest feats of arms by soldiers of any nationality throughout the war. Even the 4th Indian Division, with its superb reputation in North Africa and Italy, admired these American fighting men.

As a contribution to the third battle, there was another air raid on 15 March, by USAAF squadrons based in Italy, Sicily, North Africa and England. It began at 0830 hrs and lasted three and a half hours. During that time, 300 B17s dropped over 1000 tons and some 200 B25s dropped approximately 500 tons. Some bombs fell on Venafro, fifteen miles away, and caused 140 civilian casualties. Some fell among the Royal Artillery, who suffered forty-four casualties. Some fell on a Moroccan field hospital, where forty were killed and wounded. Some fell on Eighth Army Headquarters. Luckily for General Leese, the Commander, he was not in his caravan, which was wrecked.

Autumn came to Italy and with it the early darkness that is so often the cause of mistakes. A Beaufighter squadron that had earned a resounding reputation in the desert for its attacks against enemy armour, troop concentrations, artillery positions, strong points and airfields, was operating from north-east Italy. Its present rôle was anti-shipping patrols and strikes over the Adriatic, which meant much low flying – twenty feet above the sea was nothing out of the ordinary. A lot of its work lay among the Jugoslav Archipelago, where its aircraft were often under the cross-fire of flak batteries on two islands between which they had to fly.

The Germans operated two hospital ships, *Tubingen* and *Gradisca*, between Piraeus and Trieste. They had to give forty-eight hours' warning of their sailing and keep their lights on at night. They were allowed to carry only sick or wounded troops. Periodically the Royal Navy stopped them and a party went aboard to search. Sometimes they found reinforcements for the Italian Front aboard, sometimes weapons and ammunition, sometimes all three.

One evening *Gradisca* was reported by an aircraft of another squadron to be well up the Adriatic, presumably on her way to Trieste. Not having given the statutory notice of her movements, she was fair game and under suspicion of de-liberate concealment. The conclusion was that she must have able-bodied troops or a cargo of munitions and arms aboard. The decision about what action to take lay with the group captain commanding the station from which the Beaufighters operated. He ordered the squadron to intercept the vessel.

The Beau was the most heavily armed fighter of the war, with four 20mm cannon, six .303 machine guns and eight sixty-pound rockets. The squadron had already sunk the

S.S. Rex, pride of the Italian merchant fleet, the nation's biggest and most luxurious liner, when she was carrying German troops in the northern Adriatic. All it took was a salvo of rockets from each of twelve aircraft.

It was last light when they found the hospital ship and there was no time, even though they recognized her, for finesse. They repeated their previous performance and, like *Rex*, she was left mostly submerged on a sandbank. Unlike the liner, she was on an innocent mission. The German authorities who had failed to give notice of her passage were to blame for the drastic action.

Meanwhile in Britain the preparations for the Normandy landings entailed some goings-on that were more than a little bizarre in the eyes of the aircrew involved.

One of these was a Lancaster pilot who had completed a tour of bomber operations, on which he had won a DFC. This was followed by the mandatory rest of at least six months. Most men found it boring, missed the comradeship of squadron life and the close relationship with their own crew, and were impatient to return for another tour. Many pilots who spent this time as instructors complained wryly that it was more dangerous to fly with inexperienced pupils than against the enemy. The length of rest depended much on one's air crew category. The casualty rate for air gunners being the highest, these could usually count on the minimum. By 1944 the training of pilots in Canada, the USA and South Africa as well as in England was so well established that newly qualified pilots were a glut in the market. Some who were posted to squadrons had to act as flight engineers: which necessitated a pilot's knowledge of the engines and fuel systems and the ability to fly and land an aircraft if its pilot were killed or badly wounded.

This particular pilot, having passed an instructors' course on which he was assessed 'Above the Average' had more difficulty than most in returning to operations. Eventually, he was offered a posting to a Lancaster squadron that towed gliders and would be in action on D-Day. He accepted it glumly. His depression was deepened when he arrived at the station, where he expected to find a large airfield with Lancasters and gliders dispersed around the perimeter. There was no airfield. The place had been a basic training camp, where recruits were sent to do drill and physical training.

He was issued with a khaki battledress, Army boots and gaiters and found that he had to undergo infantry training. The logic of this was not evident until he was told that he would not be flying Lancs after all, but the aircraft that they towed. The sop of towing gliders as the only available operational alternative to a second bombing tour, especially as P Staff, who decided postings, had not been candid with him, was like offering vinegar to a man who thirsted for a pint of bitter. When a Lancaster released its glider, it returned to base. But once the glider was released, its pilot had to stay where he landed it. This meant that all RAF glider pilots had to fight alongside their soldier passengers.

The RAF squad found that the Army officer instructing them in the use of mortars had a warped sense of humour. Having let them practise firing one, he decided that it would be instructive for them to experience mortar fire from a different aspect. Without telling them why, he sent them at the double to the middle of a distant field. When they arrived there breathless and sweating, they wondered, as they sat down and lit cigarettes, what was the object of the exercise. They learned when they heard half a dozen mortars fired and saw their shells rise. They watched the shells arc towards them. They rose hastily to their feet and scattered, uncertain where the missiles would fall. The nearest landed within thirty yards, but instead of exploding it emitted a belch of smoke. As one of them complained, even a smoke bomb could do a man a grave mischief if it hit him.

The former Lancaster pilot was soon extricated from his uncongenial occupation and prospects. Thanks to some Staff officer waking up to the fact that as an operational pilot as well as instructor he had been highly assessed, he was presently flying a Mosquito in the Pathfinder Force.

★   ★   ★

Night flying during the weeks immediately preceding the invasion of France was fraught with the possibilities of misidentification. A pilot on patrol in a night fighter Mosquito was listening to an American night fighter pilot from the same station, in a P61 Black Widow, being vectored on to a target by a ground controller. Presently he heard: 'I'm gonna shoot the bastard down' and bullets hammered into his port engine, which stopped. While successfully taking evasive action, he heard the same voice announce that the 'Hun' was going down in flames.

The night of 5/6 June was highly productive of wild gunnery. Allied ships of every kind had been, throughout the war, dedicated to the principle of 'shoot first and identify afterwards' whenever an aircraft came in sight or was picked up by the human ear, sound detectors or radar. Armed merchant vessels, from the smallest fishing boat to the biggest liners, were as great a menace to aircrew as the conventional warships. On this night, there was a considerable presence of the United States Navy in the English Channel – as trigger-happy a gauntlet as any aeroplane could have to run.

The Lancaster of No 15 Squadron in which Flight Sergeant Douglas Schofield was the bomb aimer was crossing the Channel on its return to Mildenhall from an operation. Abruptly, the thoughts of the crew were diverted from contemplation of the hot meal awaiting them after de-briefing to the urgent business of self-preservation.

Schofield says, 'It was around three in the morning and pitch dark. We were already beginning to lose altitude on what should have been a quiet night. Suddenly, without warning, all hell broke loose below and flak came up at us from the sea. At least two Lancasters were shot down in our view. A terrible thing to happen, because when we gave this information at the de-briefing, they [the Intelligence officers] had no clues. It was only then that we found out that 'D' Day had just started. That morning we were informed that the US Navy was to blame; they got their codes wrong or something like that. An apology came through from the Head of the US Navy about five days later. In the meantime, two fine crews had been lost. I mention two aircraft, but as we were usually kept in the dark about everything, it might have been more.'

It was after the Normandy landings on D-Day, 6 June, 1944, that amicidal accidents multiplied most rapidly. The USAAF opened the ball with a danse macabre when 480 medium bombers emptied their bomb bays, thinking they were over Omaha Beach. General Omar Bradley, commanding the 12th Army Group, described the mission bluntly but mildly as 'completely ineffective'. The 1285 tons of bombs fell far inland, on to civilians and farm animals.

On that first morning there was a further demonstration of things to come that was a warped reflection of Dr Johnson's description of a second marriage as 'the triumph of hope over experience'. A means for tanks to become amphibious had been devised – the fitting of a waterproof canvas skirt and a propeller. From one landing ship the first thirty-two were launched too far from the beach and in rougher water than envisaged. In succession, twenty-seven of them sank. Nobody in command gave the order to halt the operation. Each crew saw its predecessors die. All concerned hoped that the experience of those who had gone before would not be repeated when they took their chance. They were literally doomed to be disillusioned.

As had happened during the landings in southern Italy, uproar and chaos bred perplexity which, in turn, sometimes led to panic. In this mood, men shoot at anyone of whose identity they are uncertain; and, on occasion, as deliberately at someone whom they recognize as a 'friend'. A Canadian soldier recalls that a rifleman whom he recognized as American kept shooting at him under the impression that he was a German. 'It was him or me, so I shot that boy even though I knew he was a Yank.' This must have happened dozens of times during those days of close combat in country abounding with thick hedgerows and woodland, in all the armies engaged.

Even when the battle moved on, everyone's nerves were tense. Air Vice Marshal J.E.J. 'Johnny' Johnson, DSO and two bars, DFC and bar, who was Group Captain commanding 125 (Spitfire) Wing, has described what happened at one of the forward airstrips to which his wing moved. There were still snipers about, so everyone was wary. One of the aircraftmen, taking a stroll around, went into an abandoned enemy pillbox, where he found some discarded German uniforms. To entertain his mates he put one on, went outside and called out to them. Nobody recognized him. Taking no chances, one of them shot him dead.

People guilty of causing accidents through carelessness are apt to attribute them to hallucination – anything but an admission of their own obtuseness or inefficiency. It is odd how young men whom their Squadron Medical Officers rate as sound in body and mind, and who have never flirted with the supernatural or suffered from a visual aberration, see things that aren't there.

It happened one night over Belgium. The Control and Reporting System had identified an aircraft as hostile. A controller at a Ground Controlled Interception radar station in France was vectoring the pilot and radar operator of a Beaufighter night fighter on to it. When they closed to visual distance it was flying at 1000 ft. They 'saw' that it wore invasion stripes – broad white bands on the upper and lower surfaces of both wings, which identified Allied aircraft to their own air, land and sea forces.

They assumed that, since it was apparently a JU188, it must be trying to pass itself off as British or American while it went about some secret nefarious mission. So they shot it down.

The Squadron Intelligence Officer was rather dubious, so he tested the accuracy of the crew's aircraft identification. He showed them silhouettes of a Ju88, a Ju188, a He111, a Mosquito and a Wellington. They consistently claimed that the one they had seen was a Ju188.

This was sustained until the next day, when all the night's operations were examined and missing aircraft accounted for.

An intruder Mosquito had faded from the radar coverage in the place where, and at the time when, the 'Ju188' was shot down. There was the fresh wreckage of a Mosquito at the scene.

Shades of 6 September, 1939. Just as the early radar equipment of that time and the inexperience of all concerned had led to Hurricanes and Spitfires being misidentified as hostile, so the current system had wrongly marked the Mosquito as an enemy aircraft. The Beaufighter crew were nevertheless to blame for poor aircraft identification and the pilot for not discussing the invasion stripes with the controller before firing his four cannon and six machine guns.

The gallantry, power of leadership and other great qualities possessed by Air Chief Marshal Sir Harry Broadhurst, KBE, CBE, DSO, DFC and bar, AFC, are as arresting as his personality. They are all the more remarkable because he won his decorations at a stage in his career when most men would consider that the opportunity had passed them by.

In 1931 he had been mentioned in despatches for operations on the North-West Frontier of India. He was a fine marksman. When commanding No 19 Squadron, he led the three-man team that won the inter-squadron Air Firing Championship in 1937. As a pilot he was also exceptional and led an aerobatic trio that gave a display with his wingtips tied to the others', at the annual Hendon Air Show. When the war began in 1939 he was thirty-three years old and commanding No 111 Squadron (Hurricanes). He shot down his first enemy aircraft, a He111, on 29 November, 1939. Although promoted to wing commander soon after, he continued flying on operations over France and in the Battle of Britain. When he became a group captain, Station Commander at Hornchurch, he still flew operational sorties.

By the time of the Commando raid on Dieppe on 19 August, 1942 he held the DSO, DFC and AFC and was Deputy Senior Air Staff Officer at No 11 Group Headquarters. He took part in planning the air cover for the raid, borrowed a Spitfire from Hornchurch and took part in it. On his first sortie he shot down a FW190. He made three more sorties, on which he damaged three hostile aeroplanes, and flew for more than eight hours that day. Between flights, he reported the battle situation, and made tactical recommendations, to the Air Officer Commanding 11 Group. In 1943 he was the youngest Air Vice Marshal on the Active List and had scored twelve confirmed victories and four probables.

In February, 1943, he had taken command of Western Desert Air Force. It was in the desert campaign during 1941 and 1942, when Air Vice Marshal Sir Arthur Coningham commanded it, that the most efficient method of close co-operation between the RAF and the Army had been devised. Sir Harry thus became well versed in the techniques of close air support for land forces during Desert Air Force's operations in Italy, where some new features were introduced. In March, 1944, therefore, he was appointed to form a new Group, No 83, in preparation for the invasion of France.

When he returned to England he took with him a light aeroplane, a Fieseler Storch, which had been captured from the Luftwaffe and was much admired by the RAF for its hardiness. Among other attractive attributes, it could take off and land in the length of a cricket pitch. The No 83 Group Communications Squadron was commanded by another strong character and outstanding fighter pilot, Squadron Leader F. W. 'Taffy' Higginson, DFC, DFM (later Wing Commander and OBE). Taffy had fifteen confirmed kills to his credit, had been shot down in France in 1941, evaded capture for some months, was caught, imprisoned, escaped and returned to England. Sir Harry entrusted the squadron with the maintenance of his precious private aeroplane, and only he and Taffy were allowed to fly it. To emphasize that this aircraft was now in British hands, it was painted the bright yellow of RAF training aircraft and bore the usual red, white and blue roundels and tail markings. Sir Harry used it for visiting radar sites and other places where there was no landing strip, as well as his airfields, and for observing during major bombing attacks.

General Sir Miles Dempsey, who had commanded an armoured division in the desert and XIII Corps in Italy, was now in command of the Second Army, which had landed in Normandy on D-Day. Caen was about to be bombed, so the General asked the AVM to take him up to watch.

The British forces in France nearly lost two of their most valuable senior officers that day. They were flying on the Allied side of the line at about three hundred feet, at the aircraft's cruising speed of some sixty knots, when anti-aircraft shells burst around them. Steel shards perforated the fuselage and wings. Sir Harry made a rapid landing while the friendly gunners kept firing. As the aircraft lost height, the guns' barrels were depressed until their crews were in danger of hitting each other. As soon as the Storch touched down, a Canadian officer with a Sten gun came charging up to capture pilot and passenger. The General's red-banded cap and the Air Vice Marshal's braid must have been a great disappointment for him.

CHAPTER 10

The chronicle of any war that lasts more than a few days is bound to be one of botched chances, unavoidable bad luck, misplaced confidence between allies and between the different armed Services. In France, the four months following the Normandy D-Day produced more of all these than any other similar period between September, 1939, and August, 1945.

In July, 1944, there were two occasions, on successive days, when the misjudgment known as 'creep back' or 'short bombing' – dropping bombs short of the target or bomb line – was committed. Five weeks after the landings, the front line ran from Lessay, on the west of the Cherbourg Peninsula, to some eight miles east of Caen. It was time to break out and Cobra was the code name for the operation that would do so. It was to open with the carpet-bombing of an area three and a half miles long and one and a half miles wide. The intention was to kill or stun the Germans on a scale that would prepare the way for a fast advance. The bomb line would be the south side of the road that ran from St Lô to Périers.

The date was 24 July and 1,600 USAAF aircraft were airborne to open the attack when rain and low cloud forced their recall. Some of the pilots obeyed the signal, others did not receive it or heard it too late and had already dropped their bombs. Among the American ground troops, 25 were killed and 131 wounded. In a fury of retaliation, many fired at the aeroplanes.

Next morning the weather was fine and at 1000 hrs the USAAF tried again. This time there were 1,800 heavy bombers on the job. General Omar Bradley, commanding the American forces in Normandy, had asked them to make their bombing run from east to west, parallel with the bomb line. He should have been able to take this for granted: obviously it was the only safe line of approach to avoid bombing his troops. Instead they came in from north to south. The enemy's heavy 88mm flak put up a dense barrage. Soon parachutes and burning aircraft were seen in the sky. The ground force's positions were marked with yellow panels, but the airmen were too high to spot them. The first wave of bombers dropped red smoke flares as an aiming mark. The smoke from these mingled with the smoke from the bursting bombs. The following aircraft began to bomb the drifting smoke, which a five-knot breeze was carrying across the bomb line to the Allied side. In the ensuing shambles, although enormous casualties and the loss of tanks, guns and vehicles were inflicted on the enemy, 101 Americans, among them Lieutenant-General McNair, who had come from Washington specially to see the troops attack, were killed and 463 wounded.

On 7 August the USAAF jettisoned part of their bomb load on to the 51st (Highland) Division, killed some sixty of them and wounded about 300.

Then, on 8 August, came Operation Totalise, when the British 2nd Army thrust towards Falaise. For the first time ever, heavy bombers operating by night were to support the Army in attack. The Air Officer Commanding-in-Chief of the RAF components of the Expeditionary Force, Sir Trafford Leigh-Mallory, explained that the usual procedure could not be followed. When bombing close to troops, the method called first for the use of 'Oboe', a radar aid to navigation. The Pathfinder Oboe Marker, having thus located the target, dropped a marker. The rest of the Pathfinder Force dropped more markers. The Master Bomber then went in low enough to identify the target visually. On confirming it, he ordered 'Bombs Away' and the heavies dropped their loads.

Bomber Command was prepared to carry out the task, using coloured concentrations as aiming marks. It would first have to be proved to the satisfaction of the Master Bombers concerned that red or green concentrations of marker shells from twenty-five pounder guns could be clearly identified at night. A practice was carried out that night on the 1st British Corps front and found satisfactory.

The RAF's bombardment at 2300 hrs on 7 August was impeccable. All 4,500 tons of bombs dropped that night fell in the target area. At 2330 hrs, armour and infantry set off on the attack, their way lit by searchlights.

At dawn all objectives had fallen to the advancing force and counter-attacks had been fought off. Typhoons and Spitfires flew sweeps along the roads in the enemy-held area. Shortly before 1300 hrs on the 8th, the good spirits of the British, Canadians and Poles turned to outrage.

The USAAF attacked that afternoon. The same method of marking was used as for the RAF fourteen hours before. The Americans made their runs through intense and accurate flak, which shot down nine of them. Their bombing was well concentrated on three of the four areas, but one could not be positively identified and only one aircraft bombed it. Altogether 492 of the 678 bombers on the mission actually bombed.

Twenty-four B17s dropped 90,000 lbs of fragmentation bombs on the Polish Armoured Division and 3rd Canadian Infantry Division, killed 86 and wounded 376. They also demolished seven guns and 83 vehicles.

There is no public record of disciplinary action taken against the erring crew members.

Only once was the RAF guilty of a bombing error that played havoc among friendly forces on a gigantic scale. Operation Tractable, on 14 August, was a massive attack on Falaise, in which the Canadian 2nd Corps took part. Of the 417 Lancasters, 352 Halifaxes and forty-two Mosquitoes in support, 300 aircraft were from Canadian squadrons. The target was Quesnay Wood, held by a strong enemy force. The Pathfinders were, for once, careless, made a four-mile navigation error and marked the wrong wood.

The RAF does not tolerate inefficiency. A Court of Inquiry blamed certain pilots and navigators. Two Pathfinder crews were posted to ordinary bomber crew duties. Some squadron and flight commanders were reduced in rank and office and also posted back to Bomber Command's main force. All crews implicated were suspended from operations within thirty miles of the forward bomb line until reassessed after further experience.

There was a compounding factor that aggravated the bombing error. Through inefficient liaison between the Army and RAF Staffs, these aircraft used target indicators which, as usual, emitted yellow smoke. The ground troops always used yellow smoke flares to indicate their position to friendly aircraft of the 2nd Tactical Air Force, which had been formed specifically for the invasion and was based in France. They did so now, to warn their errant friends: but these aircraft did not belong to 2nd TAF, they were from Canadian Squadrons of Bomber Command and based in England, so assumed that they were seeing Pathfinder Force target indicators and bombed accordingly. British anti-aircraft guns tried to discourage them, without noticeable effect. The holocaust cost the Canadians 112 dead, 376 injured, 265 vehicles, thirty guns and two tanks.

While this was happening, a pilot baled out of his Typhoon when it was hit by ground fire near Falaise. As he descended under his parachute, another member of his squadron strafed the flak gunners to prevent them shooting at him. This was not entirely successful, but despite ground fire aimed at him, he landed unhurt. He was immediately seized and tied to a tree. His captors were about to shoot him when an officer turned up and stopped them. Instead, they put him in a lorry that was part of a convoy. His life was not yet out of danger: another Typhoon, from his own squadron, attacked the lorry and he was lucky not to be hit.

A pilot in a different Typhoon squadron had to bale out when his aeroplane was hit by light flak and caught fire. He suffered burns on the arms and face and hurt his leg on the tail plane. On landing, he saw men waving to him, thought they were French, so limped towards them. They were the enemy and he was soon lying on the floor of an ambulance. With him were four German soldiers on stretchers. To avoid being strafed by the RAF and USAAF, the Germans had been putting Red Cross flags on the roofs of lorries. General Eisenhower had ordered that pilots must not fire at these except in return if fired on. Neither airmen, soldiers nor sailors are inclined to obey orders blindly, particularly when given by a commander who is not – and, in this instance, had never been – in action himself. A Spitfire shot up the lorry with its 20mm cannon. The Typhoon pilot was wounded in the legs and shoulders. He never found out whether any of the other passengers survived. The enemy treated him well: after attending to his injuries, they left him in a town from which they were retreating, to be picked up by the advancing Allies.

During those days when the fighting around Falaise was confused, Typhoons and USAAF P47 fighter-bombers made many attacks on Canadian and Polish infantry and tanks, during which the Poles shot down at least one Typhoon.

The 18th of August was another day of great amicidal execution by Allied fighter-bombers using rockets, cannon and machine guns. Over forty incidents were reported, in which there were fifty-one casualties to troops and twenty-five vehicles were destroyed.

These were abominable ways in which to die or be injured, but they were of the kind that men expect to have to face. There were many others, even more tragic because so unexpected, that also took many lives and inflicted horrible injuries. Throughout, since the first wave of Allied troops went ashore, freakish mishaps had been killing and maiming.

Times uncounted, crews sleeping under their tanks for protection from shells and wet weather had the life crushed out of them when the tanks sank into soft soil. The Sten gun was a fine weapon, but crudely mass-produced and dangerous when handled roughly. It was known for infantrymen sleeping with a Sten beside them to be shot when, in the dark, someone stepped on it. Hand grenades fused for four seconds sometimes detonated in a fraction of that time and blew the thrower's head off. Soldiers lost a leg or foot by straying on to ground where their own side had laid mines, others tripped and impaled themselves on their own bayonets. The undertones of war are as horrible in their unexpected, stealthy way as the overt brutality of its great booming chords.

A massive dramatic spectacle, one of the most savage and shameful in the long list of inter-Service bungling, was enacted on 27 August, 1944. It had all the ingredients of high tragedy: misplaced trust, the dutiful execution of an order that the commander who had to obey it mistrusted, the infliction of violent death and injury on brothers in arms.

Although the Allies had advanced beyond Paris, Le Havre was still in enemy hands. Allied ships at anchor in harbour or on the open sea were nightly targets for E-boats and midget submarines. All day British minesweepers swept a clear passage for friendly shipping. For the past few days one flotilla of these, six in number, had been sweeping a minefield near Le Havre. This was a mission of particular importance – its purpose, to enable a battleship and two other big warships to shell Le Havre.

On 26 August, during a twenty-four-hour rest, the captain of *HMS Jason*, the flotilla leader, a regular officer, was ordered to revert on the next day to a previous task: sweeping the Channel between Portsmouth and Arromanches. This had been given priority, so the premature diversion to another area puzzled him. He sent his navigating officer to the Headquarters Ship to query it. There, this officer was assured that the order would be changed so that the flotilla could finish its former commitment.

The Headquarters ship should immediately have signalled the alteration to the flotilla. All activity of Allied ships off the French coast had to be notified in advance to the other Services, so the signal should have been sent also to their various Headquarters. Among the addressees who ought to have been informed was the Flag Officer British Assault Area, a Rear-Admiral.

The flotilla received its new orders on the next day, shortly before it was time to sail. Only four ships, *Jason*, *Britomart*, *Salamander* and *Hussar*, did so: one had been damaged by a mine and the engine of another was being repaired. Two trawlers accompanied them to lay dan buoys to mark the swept channels. In the early afternoon *Hussar*'s gear developed a fault and she had to stop sweeping but remained with the others. It was a hot, sunny day and men off watch were sunbathing.

At 1330 hrs the ships' crews heard aeroplanes approaching at high speed. Streaks of smoke spurted from beneath their wings as missiles hurtled towards the little ships.

The wing commander commanding the Typhoon squadron that made the attack had been flying Typhoons since he joined his first squadron in 1942. By the time he led his present squadron into an assault on the Royal Navy he held the DFC and bar and had scored sixteen and a half confirmed victories, which remained the highest achieved by any Typhoon pilot. He went on to win the DSO and AFC and rise to be a group captain.

He had been astonished when ordered to take off on this operation: it was well known that British minesweepers had been working near Le Havre for the past week. When airborne, he had asked his Ground Controller for confirmation of the target and was told that the ships were definitely German. When he sighted them he queried this assurance and was given the same answer. When he closed the ships he once more expressed his doubts. Told again to carry on as instructed, he had no choice but to obey the order.

The Typhoon was armed with four 20mm cannon and either eight sixty-pound rockets or two 1000 lb bombs. Perhaps it would have been a slightly less hideous day for the Navy if these had had bombs slung beneath them. Rockets were much easier to aim and their effect was appalling.

Immediately the aircraft opened fire, *Jason* reported the fact by wireless to her Headquarters. Two minutes later her captain saw that two minesweepers had been hit and were heeling over. The fighters swept round for a second run and *Jason* fired the correct recognition signals. The reply was a burst of cannon shells. Rockets had set *Salamander* alight. *Britomart* and *Hussar* were also burning. One of the trawlers, *Colsay*, had stopped. *Jason* had returned the attackers' fire with her two Oerlikons and now reported to HQ that the burning ships were in danger of sinking.

The Typhoons came in for a second run. Eleven minutes after their first salvoes they flew away.

Two of the ships that had caught fire were sinking and the third was listing badly. Men, some of them wounded, were in the water among flotsam and dead bodies. One sweeper sent its motor launch away to pick up survivors, but cannon shells had made holes in it and it sank after hauling a few aboard.

One sweeper turned turtle before going down. Fourteen of her officers and ratings had been killed and more than seventy wounded. Another went down by the stern. Fifty-three of her officers and ratings died and thirty-nine were wounded.

About a quarter of an hour after the attack began, an RAF air-sea rescue high speed launch arrived and began taking men from the water. She was presently joined by two minesweepers. One of the trawlers had suffered six casualties, but she was able to help with the work of rescue.

Altogether, seventy-eight of all ranks were killed and 149 wounded. The uninjured and those wounded who were fit to travel were taken to England two days later. After being interrogated, they were warned not to say a word about anything that had happened.

The first reaction of those who had been aboard the unlucky ships had, naturally, been to blame the RAF. Inquiries made it clear that the Navy was entirely to blame. Naval Headquarters had ordered the strike, because an officer on the staff of Captain Minesweepers had neglected to make sure that the signal changing the order about where the minesweepers were to do their work on 27 August was repeated to the Flag Officer British Assault Area.

An hour and a half before the Navy asked for the attack an RAF reconnaissance aircraft had overflown the ships and reported them as friendly. It has to be assumed that either the Navy was not informed of this or was given the information and disbelieved it.

Three senior naval officers were court-martialled. Two were acquitted and the third was reprimanded. The actual culprit, who forgot to warn all those concerned, deserved to be whipped round the Fleet, as he would have been in Nelson's day – if he were a rating.

The Ardennes is a forested range of hills, on both sides of the River Meuse, which stretches from France into Belgium and Luxembourg. The Germans had come that way when they invaded France in May, 1940. Four and a half years later it was the opinion of General Eisenhower, Supreme Allied Commander, that an advance across it was impossible, or at best a reluctant choice, for both the Allies and the Germans. He therefore put only six US divisions to defend it on a seventy-mile front that extended from Malmédy in Belgium to Trier in Germany. Hitler ordered an assault on the Ardennes by twenty divisions, eleven of them armoured, with five in reserve. Allied Intelligence did not know or suspect this. The Germans attacked on 16 December, 1944, in foggy weather with ten-tenths cloud cover. The Americans fought well, but the enemy gained ground. By the 19th the Belgian town of Bastogne, held by the US 101st Airborne Division, was cut off and surrounded by German armour thrusting for the Meuse.

The weather improved enough on the 23rd to enable the USAAF to make a contribution in aid of their buddies on the ground. Their target was in Germany – Zulpich, a railhead for the German Army. The twenty-eight bombers were B26 Marauders. When they reached time-on-target, most of the pilots and navigators recognized that they were off course: some aborted the mission, others attacked alternative targets. Six of their number were not bright enough to know they were not where they were meant to be, so dropped their loads and, on return to base, reported 'excellent results'. There was some divergence of opinion about this. Headquarters 30th US Division had telephoned US 1st Army HQ to complain, 'Our guys are bombing Malmédy and we don't have any telephone lines to there left.'

Malmédy is in Belgium, thirty-three miles from Zulpich. Its small fire brigade was unable to cope with the great blaze that the bombs had ignited in the town centre. High explosive, raging flames and the crushing weight of falling buildings killed and injured dozens of civilians and American soldiers.

American military engineers hastened there. They were still digging survivors out of the rubble on the afternoon of Christmas Eve, when eighteen B24 Liberators appeared in the sky and dropped their bombs. The fires, the damage to buildings and the casualties exceeded those of the previous day.

On Christmas Day the rescue work was not yet finished when thirty-six B26s arrived overhead on their way to bomb St Vith, which the Germans had occupied. Four mistook Malmédy for this target and bombed it, causing more ruination, more deaths, more injuries.

Total casualties over the three days were at least 125 civilians killed and an unknown number wounded, thirty-seven Americans killed and about 100 wounded.

CHAPTER 11

In January, 1945, the markings of the Second Tactical Air Force's aircraft had to be changed. Air Marshal Sir Arthur Coningham, KCB, DSO, MC, DFC, AFC, Air Officer Commanding 2nd TAF, was forced to take this precaution. Seven months after the Normandy landings Allied anti-aircraft gunners, the RAF itself and the most frequent offenders, the USAAF, were still failing to identify them as friendly. It was thought that the new markings would be easy to recognize.

Spinners★ were painted black. A white ring was inserted between the red and blue ones on the wing upper surfaces and this whole new roundel was outlined in yellow. The D-Day stripes below the fuselage were obliterated. The rear fuselage 'sky' bands were also painted out – the Luftwaffe had similar markings.

Despite this, in late March Typhoons were still being harassed by ack-ack, USAAF P47s (Thunderbolts) and P51s (Mustangs) and, rarely but disgracefully, by Spitfires. An Australian pilot whose nose tank was hit – for a change – by enemy flak was returning to his airstrip when flak hit him again. He lost four feet off a wing and all his Glycol coolant, without which his engine would soon seize. Some P47s chose this moment to try to shoot him down and he was lucky to make a forced landing and survive with his life.

★The nose-cone or boss on a propeller.

Three days later another Typhoon had to crash-land short of fuel, thanks to being forced into a fight with P51s.

Enemy aircrew underwent the same kinds of nuisance as the RAF. Leutnant Heinz Ewald, who ended the war with 84 kills to his credit, had his problems. The Luftwaffe's operational strength had dwindled to the point where Generalleutnant Adolf Galland, who had been in command of the entire fighter force since November, 1941, when he was only 29, had returned to full-time operational flying in January, 1945. By then he had scored 104 victories.

Ewald's account of one of his own sorties in March, 1945, is good-natured in the universal easy-going fighter pilot style.

'The alarm sounded and we started engines: Edi Pitzl, Gerd Hauter, Anton Kellmeier. In the Stuhlweissenburg area, the Russians were attacking and the air was thick with German heavy flak.

' "Attention! Lots of Red Indians [code for enemy aircraft] ahead," I called.

' "Holy Moses, Esau [his nickname and callsign]," I thought, "here come at least twenty Silver Birds with their black American stars on the wings and fuselage."

'I called Edi, "You and your wing man climb above them and make the first attack. We'll separate now."

'A section of these boys from overseas are bound to turn back at full belt. Paul Slodczyk, my wing man, is keeping good attack formation and we're steering north-west to peel off and dive on to the Americans.

'During the climb I call "Jumbo", our Operations Room, and report several Americans, in the hope that they will send up some more pairs of fighters. Four against more than twenty! Fighting against superior numbers was our daily lot – the same today. Now the "Amis" were flying over the Plattensee at about 2800 metres. They were approaching our airfield. Apparently they weren't worried by us, which didn't please me. I held the climb until we were about 1500 metres higher and the boys were slanted below us.

'As I called "Attack!" to my Number Two, I winged

over and dived into action. At the same instant Edi Pitzl on my left swooped on a Mustang.

'Yes, he had scored a hit. A Silver Bird was spinning down on fire and a parachute was drifting to the ground. While I confirmed his kill and congratulated him, my Silver Bird appeared in my sights. I yelled to Esau 2, "Shoot at the outside right – check your aim with a quick squirt." We went for the Mustangs straight and level . . . much closer, so much the better – now press the firing button. My first burst unfortunately went wide because I didn't allow enough deflection and also because he slanted down at the same moment. My wing man's shot was also ineffectual. My Messerschmitt was in a vertical bank and we curved flat out. I was not in a shooting position but I kept my opponent in the gunsight. Suddenly tracer came at us from ahead and from several directions. Damn, it was not harmless. A mad American had joined our carousel as we whirled around. The shooter might easily hit one of his friends. I thought this wild shooter probably came from Texas and was used to shooting at whisky glasses in saloons. He must have got in a lucky shot, because my engine began to spew oil and vibrate.

'The Mustang pilot turned and turned, then two Messerschmitt boys sat on his neck. He turned his machine so tightly and fast that its wings also vibrated. His machine dipped under us and I fired at it once. Again he had to turn. A renewed burst of fire from my guns. It shot past him once more. Then the Ami abruptly went into a diving turn. With split-second reaction, I followed and got closer, but my Messerschmitt started vibrating again. I fired two bursts. The Mustang was hit. My shots must have damaged his steering gear. The Silver Bird held a gentle turn and I fired for the last time and hit it in the fuselage and wings. As I pulled away, I missed ramming my winger by a hair's breadth, there was an explosion in the Mustang's engine cowling, bits flew off it and the Mustang began to burn, leaving a brown trail behind it as it made a shallow dive towards the ground.

'The Americans were circling like watchful hyenas at a respectful distance and, thank God, had not been able to share in the fight because of the wild shooter. But now, faced with the burning aircraft – the death torch – more than half of them turned westwards towards safety at full throttle. Edi was not pleased by this as it deprived him of the chance to score another success.

'The rest of the Americans were coming closer, climbing slowly. My winger and I rushed westwards at full boost and with a well-judged turn put ourselves in a new position up-sun. Meanwhile I counted the Americans, who must have had plenty of petrol aboard and, dammit, not all of them wanted to scram. There were still nine of them circling near our airfield like startled chickens. They looked as though they were watching for the chance to pounce on aircraft taking off or landing. We would have to land when our fuel gave out and my red light had come on, which meant that I had only ten minutes' endurance left. I told my No. 2 to turn north, dive to the deck and make for an airfield about thirty kilometres away.

'I wanted to make another brave dash at the Amis, but my engine was chucking out oil, faltering and vibrating. The revs were dropping. I told myself I had to make an emergency landing, so turned south towards the Plattensee and the town of Vescprem with my engine making increasingly distressing noises. I was approaching the high ground on which the bishop's palace stood. Light German flak came past me and then high explosive shells began to burst around me.

'On the airfield 120 gun barrels of various calibres of flak were pointed my way. I jettisoned the cockpit canopy, unbuckled the straps and threw myself out on the left side, hitting my knee. I pulled the ripcord and in a few seconds was dangling under the parachute at 150 metres, thank God. I landed about 400 metres from the airfield, but the odyssey wasn't over. Hungarian workmen swinging pick-axes and shovels were running towards me, shouting "Kill the Russian!" as I lay on my back. I drew my pistol and began shooting like someone in a Wild West film, over their heads.

'A car came dashing up, driven by my friend Sachsenberg,

who had scored 104 victories. He called out, "Dear old Esau, first our own flak shoots at you, then German infantry with assault weapons, then our Hungarian allies with pickaxes to bash your head in! You've been thrice lucky – typical of you!"

'The American pilot whom Edi Pitzl had shot down was a Sergeant Wuws from Chicago. He had baled out and spent half the day with us. The Squadron Medical Officer treated him for light burns. We talked about our fight, we in our school English, and about the madness of war. He said we were good fellows, but why did we want to kill him? We didn't answer him with the same question! *C'est la guerre*, that's war.'

In February there had been a rare instance of amicide by tank crews.

The US 30th Division was gaining ground in Germany along the River Roer, where the country was flat and open, offering poor cover for operations by day. Each advance from one town or village to another had to be made at night. An attack by the US 117th Infantry was planned for the night of 26/27 February, after due daytime reconnaissance and planning. The 3/117 was to move up from Steinstrass and pass between the 2/117 and 1/117, then attack on the left at 2230 hrs to capture Kleintroisdorf. The 1/117 would attack at the same time on the right and take Kirchtroisdorf. After this the 2/117 would be committed through the 3/117, with Putz as the objective. The infantry would be supported by 'B' and 'C' Companies of the 743 US Tank Battalion; and flail tanks of 'A' Troop, 1st Lothian and Border Horse, a Yeomanry regiment, to breach minefields.

The assault began at 2230 hrs. By midnight Kirchtroisdorf had fallen to the 1/117 and Kleintroisdorf to the 3/117. At 0300 hrs on the 27th the 2/117 moved ahead as planned and seized Putz.

The four Yeomanry tanks assigned to follow the 1/117 when they attacked on the right towards Kirchtroisdorf strayed left into the zone of the 3/117. After covering several hundred yards the commander of the leading one realized his mistake and about-turned. The 3/117 and its accompanying armour, Company B of the 743rd Tank Battalion and another four of A Troop 1st Lothian and Border Horse, had jumped off ten minutes late. They saw the four strayed tanks when these approached the 3/117's line of advance. Assuming, because of the direction from which they were coming, that these must be German, they opened fire and wiped them all out.

Harry Ashley was an RAF official photographer who flew on many operations in Lancasters, Mosquitoes and Dakotas over Germany, France and Burma without injury. It was on his only sortie over enemy territory in a training type that he came to grief.

On 14 February, 1945, he took off from a jungle airstrip at 0630 hrs in a Harvard piloted by Flying Officer Jackson of No 152 Squadron. His purpose was to photograph the smoke screen laid over the Irrawaddy River to cover the 14th Army crossing. The squadrons based in that wild country were unable to observe the strict procedure that was standard in more civilized surroundings. The decision to make the flight was taken at the last moment and Harry doubts that any other squadrons had been notified of the mission or time of take-off. The St Valentine's Day surprise he was about to receive was equally unorthodox.

Two Spitfires of No 17 Squadron, which was commanded by Squadron Leader J. H. Lacey, DFM and bar, appeared – a reassuring sight, even though the Japanese often flew captured British aircraft.

He recalls, 'I remember the Spitfire coming astern of us and suddenly Jacko slumped over the controls and I saw blood oozing through his helmet. Although there was a hole right through my arm, I felt no pain and had no idea that I had been hit until after we landed and I found my sleeve soaked in blood.

'The force of air in descent brought the pilot to consciousness. Pulling back the stick he glided us down and our landing was cushioned by some tall grasses. We disembarked very quickly and discovered that a shell fragment had cut open Jacko's helmet, cut the skin and stunned him. As we walked away, he said "We ought to have a picture", so we returned for me to photograph him kneeling on the wing.' An admirable display of British *sang froid*.

The Group Operations Room had warned the fighter squadrons to keep a look-out for low-flying enemy aircraft. The Harvard, which was cruising at 500 ft, had a radial engine, as did Japanese machines. The Spitfire pilot, Flying Officer D. W. Rathwell, DFC, a Canadian, mistook it for a Nakajima Ki-43 Hayabusa, code-named 'Oscar'. His short burst of cannon fire before he realized his error used only sixteen rounds, all of which hit the Harvard. All Ginger Lacey's pilots had to fly and shoot to a high standard, or he sent them back to the pool.

Blue Section, Rathwell and his No 2, had been patrolling at 2000 ft, while Green Section patrolled at 20,000 ft. The two section leaders had a small wager on which of them would be the first to shoot down a Jap. Green Leader was thinking about this when he heard Blue Leader call excitedly, 'I've got one, Green One.' Then, after a short pause, 'Bollocks, it's a Harvard.'

With aircraft operating near their frontiers, neutral countries could not take it for granted that their peace would be undisturbed. The people of Zürich have a reputation for cold, austere smugness that is largely the product of envy for their prosperous, secure way of life and beautiful city. There is no reason why opulence and a comfortably ordered existence should not be accompanied by a sense of humour. Native Zürcher wit is sharp, and was much exercised, though wryly, after an event that occurred on the night of 4 March, 1945.

Six USAAF B24s dropped their bombs there and killed five citizens, put twelve in hospital and left twenty-two entire families bereft of their homes. The excuse offered for this was a combination of navigational errors, bad weather over

France, mist over Switzerland and unserviceable equipment in the aircraft.

Sometimes the grim physical and psychological consequences of friendly fire are mercifully tempered by potentially lethal incidents that are amusing rather than mortifying. Sometimes it is the uniquely British quality of wry deprecation that makes a dangerous moment appear cause for no more than mild irritation.

Of the first kind, a day on India's North-West Frontier in 1937 comes to mind. The 2nd Battalion of the 4th Prince of Wales's Own Gurkha Rifles had been in a large-scale battle against Pathan tribesmen, who were a formidable enemy and fighting on their home ground. Fine marksmen, wielders of long-bladed, sharp-pointed knives, fanatically brave, although they fought like fiends and were cruel to prisoners and the wounded, they regarded war as a sport.

The Gurkhas were as brave, trained riflemen, notorious for their deadly skill with the kukri, their heavy, curved knife with its razor-sharp blade. Better even than a good fight they enjoyed the pursuit of game, four-legged or feathered.

This engagement with an unusually large Pathan force had involved mountain artillery, a Sikh battalion, a battalion of Highlanders and machine guns. The Gurkhas had earned the honours of the day, but suffered casualties.

'B' Company were under vicious fire from the Pathans when they were startled by bullets from a different direction that spanged off the rocks around them. One glance confirmed that these came from 'A' Company on the left, who until then had also been exchanging shots with the foe. The puzzled Gurkhas and their British Company Commander ducked while a signaller angrily wagged his flags in remonstrance. Before the offenders could reply, the reason for their dangerous shooting became clear. An oorial, a species of mountain sheep, had emerged from the rocks and scrub and was trotting across the battlefield. Instantly, also abandoning the enemy as a target, 'A' Company joined in, trying to despatch the unhappy animal before their rivals.

It was an 'A' Company Viceroy's Commission (Gurkha) officer who killed it with a fine shot at a hundred yards. Then both companies returned their attention to the secondary business of human warfare.

The second is exemplified by the experiences of a fighter pilot who was credited with seven and a half victories during the Battle of Britain and a total of fifteen by the end of the war. Air Commodore Peter Brothers, CBE, DSO, DFC, is the quintessential fighter pilot, more particularly of the pre-war vintage, with its training and attitudes: dedicated and serious about his profession, debonair, light-hearted, fizzing with high spirits and humour when at leisure. He had rather more than his fair share of involvement with bullets aimed at friendly targets.

The first episode he recalls did not involve him directly. A section of his Hurricane squadron, led by the Flight Commander, was ordered to investigate an unidentified twin-engined aeroplane over south-east England. They intercepted it and, although it bore RAF markings, shot it down. It was a Lockheed Electra, forerunner of the Hudson bomber much flown by Coastal Command at that time, which had been harmlessly employed in photographing RAF airfields so that the effectiveness of their camouflage could be examined.

Three months later Flight Lieutenant Brothers was on an offensive patrol over France when a Me109 inserted itself in the space between him and his No 2, who was on his first operation. The Messerschmitt appeared in his rear-view mirror at such short range that it blocked his view of anything else. As it opened fire, he flick half-rolled and went into a tight turn to port. He was proud to see his inexperienced No 2 cut the corner to resume his position, but less pleased when he saw the flames at the latter's gun ports. The bullets missed him and a few words on the radio put an end to the erroneous attack. When they returned to base he chided the crestfallen novice for bad shooting and took him off operations for two days' intensive gunnery training. 'He had a sitting target in me.'

On an April day in 1942, a squadron leader with a DFC

by then, he led his squadron, No 457 (Spitfires) of the Royal Australian Air Force, on an operation over France with the rest of the Kenley Wing. On the way home the Wing's squadrons had separated. When 457 were about forty miles from the Sussex coast, at 20,000 ft, they saw vapour trails made by aircraft above that were following them. These dived and opened fire as 457 broke. Their leader singled his opposite number out for his personal attention – and missed.

In return he was treated better than he deserved: 'Don't shoot,' his intended victim ordered his pilots, 'they're Spitfires.' They were 602 Squadron, also of the Kenley Wing.

One of the Australians had his own idea about the matter. 'Any bastard who shoots at me, I shoot back.' But he didn't dare disobey his C.O. and do so.

In the autumn of that year Peter Brothers took command of the Tangmere Wing and early in 1943 was awarded a bar to his DFC. One of the squadrons at Tangmere was equipped with Hurricanes and Turbinelight Havocs (a Boston variant), which operated in pairs for night fighting. The Hurricane flew 200 yards astern and to port of the Havoc, which was unarmed but fitted with a 1000 Watt light in its nose. When its radar detected a hostile aircraft ahead, the searchlight was switched on and the Hurricane pilot surged forward for the kill.

This method was not conspicuously successful, but did provide at least one victim – a Stirling bomber returning from a raid on Italy, which was shot down over Sussex. The crew baled out unhurt and were brought to the Officers' Mess at Tangmere.

Although well fed by their temporary hosts and liberally plied with peace offerings from the bar, they showed an understandable belligerence towards the Havoc crew and Hurricane pilot. Wing Commander, Flying, however, had ordered the offenders to lock themselves into their rooms and maintained the fiction that they were off the station.

CHAPTER 12

The end of the Second World War did not create the tran-
quillity envisaged in the Book of Proverbs, where wisdom
and understanding are said to bring a life whose 'ways are
pleasantness and all her paths are peace'. Neither wisdom
nor understanding was any more prominent in international
relationships after six years of conflict than before.

In 1917 the British Government had promised, through
Lord Balfour, the Foreign Secretary, to make Palestine into
a 'national home' for the Jews when the Great War should
end. This was the Balfour Declaration that has been so much
reviled by the Arab world in general and the Palestinians in
particular; and by many others, Britons included. Since 1919
Britain had governed Palestine under a mandate granted by
the League of Nations. By 1947, still under British rule, three
Jewish terrorist organizations were active: Irgun Zvai Leumi
be Eretz Israel (National Military Organization in Israel) the
biggest, which had 7000 members; Lochmei Herut Israel
(Fighters for the Freedom of Israel, also known as the Stern
Gang); and the Haganah. Their political creeds differed but
all pursued the same immediate purpose by violent means:
to rid Palestine of the British, and the Arabs if possible, and
to establish a new State to be called Israel. To this end, their
principal activity was the murder of British troops.

Until the establishment of Israel in May, 1948, Arabs and
Jews were both citizens of Palestine under British rule and
therefore technically compatriots. On 9 May, 1948, the Irgun

Zvai Leumi and the Stern Gang attacked the Arab village of Deir Yasin and massacred more than 200 inhabitants, including old women and children. Those who survived were led in a victory procession through the streets of Jerusalem in their bloodstained clothes. The purpose was to frighten the Palestinians away from their native land. It succeeded: nearly three-quarters of a million Arabs fled the country.

After the British left, the Arabs and Jews continued to be supposedly peaceful fellow-countrymen, now under their own Government. On 15 November, 1948, the people in the village of Kafr Bar'am were forced to evacuate their homes. For five years they led squalid lives as refugees in the country where they had been born. In 1953 they applied to the Supreme Court to be allowed to return to their rightful abode. The Court decided in their favour. The response was another act of friendly fire: infantry and aircraft of the Israeli Defence Army devastated the empty village, whose lands were then given to the neighbouring Jewish colonies to cultivate.

Among the Arabs there were many converts to Christianity. Kafr Qasim was a village whose inhabitants were Catholics. However, what happened there on 29 October, 1956, was not an act of 'religious cleansing' but of 'ethnic cleansing' — both terms a ludicrous and sinister misuse of the verb.

The records of the Military Court that was eventually forced to try those most responsible for the atrocity committed at Kafr Qasim, read: 'On the eve of the Sinai War a battalion was ordered to prepare itself to defend a section of the Israeli–Jordanian frontier. A unit of the Frontier Guard commanded by Major Melinki was attached to it and under the orders of the battalion commander, Brigadier Yshishkhar Shadmi. The Area Commander, Major-General Zvi Tsur, authorized the Brigadier to impose a night curfew in the villages of the minorities in the area of his command in order to facilitate the movement of his forces and to prevent the population being exposed to injury by the reserve troops.'

Among the orders that Brigadier Shadmi gave Major Melinki were to impose the curfew and implement the order for the inhabitants to remain in their houses in Kafr Qasim and seven other villages. The curfew must be extremely strict and strongly enforced. It would not be enough to arrest those who broke it – they must be shot. When Melinki asked what to do to a man returning from his work outside the village, who might meet the Frontier Guards as he entered it, the Brigadier replied, 'I don't want any sentimentality'.

Melinki briefed his officers on these and other orders, emphasizing that it was forbidden to harm inhabitants who stayed in their homes, but that anyone found outside his home or leaving it should be shot dead. He added that if a number of people were killed in the night, this would facilitate the imposition of the curfew on succeeding nights. Lieutenant Frankenthal asked what they were to do with the dead. The reply was 'They must not be removed'. A section leader, Arieh Menches, asked 'What about women and children?' The answer was, 'They must be treated like anyone else'. The minutes of this briefing bear an entry 'As from today, at 1700 hours, curfew shall be imposed in the minority villages until 0600 hours, and all who disobey this order will be shot dead'.

The officer in command of the unit that went to Kafr Qasim was Lieutenant Dahan. It was not until 1630 hrs that a Frontier Force sergeant informed the village's Mukhtar (Headman) about the curfew and warned him of the penalty for ignoring it. The Headman told him that 400 of his people worked outside the village, so he could not inform everyone of the curfew. After an argument, the sergeant promised that he would let all men returning from work pass on his own responsibility and that of the government. The Headman, assisted by his relations, announced the curfew in the centre of the village and to the north and south of it. When it came into effect half an hour after he had been notified of it, there were still dozens of people away at their places of work.

From the Court Records: 'The first to be shot at the western entrance to the village were four quarrymen returning on bicycles from the places where they worked. A short time after the curfew began these four came round a bend in the

145

road pushing their bicycles. When they had gone ten to fifteen metres along the road they were shot from behind at close range. Two were killed outright, one was wounded in the thigh and forearm, the fourth escaped by throwing himself to the ground. The bicycle of the wounded man fell on him, covering his body, and he managed to lie motionless throughout the bloody incidents that took place around him. Eventually he crawled into an olive grove and lay under a tree until morning. The man who had thrown himself to the ground was shot at again when he rolled to the roadside, whereupon he sighed and pretended to be dead. After the two massacres which took place beside him, he hid himself among a flock of sheep, whose shepherd had been killed, and escaped into the village with the flock.

'A short time after, a two-wheeled cart drawn by a mule arrived at the bend. Sitting in it were Ismail Mahmud Badir and his little daughter aged eight. Three other people walked behind or beside the cart, carrying vegetables. One of these was a boy of fourteen. At this moment Dahan arrived in the jeep with the mobile squad. Dahan ordered his men to get out of the jeep, which they did, carrying a Bren gun and two rifles. He then told Ismail to get out of the cart and stand in a row with the two men who had been walking. He told the boy to get into the cart with the little girl and drive to the village. He ordered the three men to be shot. Two were killed and one, severely wounded, was left for dead but survived.'

The next to appear were a shepherd and his twelve-year-old son, driving a flock of sheep. Both were shot dead.

The Court records continue: 'A four-wheeled cart arrived at the bend. In it was its owner, Ismail Aqqab Badir, returning from Petah Tiqva, and his cousin, Tewfiq Ibrahim Badir. Near the bend, a soldier stopped the cart, ordered the two men to get down and to stand beside it in the road. The soldier himself stood at the bend, and not far from him two other armed soldiers were lying in the road leading to the school. Immediately after the arrival of this cart, several groups of workers started arriving, riding bicycles with lighted lamps. The soldier ordered them all to lay their bicycles beside the road and stand in a row with the two men who had been in the cart. There were thirteen men in this row and when one of them, Salim Ahmad Bashir Badir, tried to stand at the end of the row, the soldier shouted to him, "Dog, stand in the middle of the row". He thereupon moved to the middle.

'When no more bicycle lamps were visible on the horizon, the same soldier asked the men standing in the row where they came from. They all answered that they were from Kafr Qasim, whereupon the soldier took a step backwards and shouted to the soldiers lying opposite the row (one of whom had a Bren gun): 'Mow them down.' All the men in the row fell under the hail of bullets that followed, except for Mustafa, who escaped by jumping over the wall. The soldiers continued firing at any of the fallen men who showed any signs of life. When it was clear that they were all dead, or almost so, the soldiers cleared the road of the bodies, piling them on the side of the road. Of these thirteen men, six were killed, while four were seriously injured.'

So the butchery continued. In the first hour the Israeli soldiers killed forty-seven Arabs, including women of all ages, one sixty-six, and seven children. Two more men were killed later.

Eleven of the killers were tried and nine found guilty. Their sentences ranged from seventeen years imprisonment for Major Melinki and fifteen for two others, to five for the rest – according to how many people they had slaughtered. These were lenient, as the penalty laid down for premeditated murder was life imprisonment.

The 1950s and 1960s were rife with military fratricide. In Korea the Americans, British and Australians were all afflicted by it. The Gloucestershire Regiment was one of the victims of misdirected artillery fire: having called for support from the guns, they found the shells falling on them instead of the true target. In Kenya British troops fighting the Mau Mau terrorists suffered three-quarters of their casualties at the hands of their comrades.

In Vietnam the Americans had to reconcile themselves in particular to being shot up or bombed by friendly aircraft, where the terrain lent itself to this kind of accident. There was a typical one on an August night in 1968 when ground troops were directing fire from a helicopter gunship. When it did open fire with rockets it killed two Americans in an armoured personnel carrier and wounded three.

A commonplace accident in Korea attributable to artillery occurred in 1967. A gun crew that should have been firing Powder Charge Seven, fired Charge Four. The shells hit an American unit where they killed one man and wounded thirty-seven. The victims called for counter-battery fire, which was all too accurate: it killed twelve and wounded forty troops at the base that had wrongly loaded its guns.

In Northern Ireland British troops patrolling in the dark occasionally clash, there is mutual shooting and someone is wounded or killed. In the wars that constantly erupt in Latin America and the Horn of Africa, doubtless the same happens. Friendly fire is sometimes deliberate. In the former Jugoslavia, Serbs and Bosnian Muslims have accused each other of deliberately firing on their own people, then pretending that it was the other side, in order to obtain sympathy from the outside world. It could well be true, particularly when one considers the unstable, intolerant natures of the peoples involved, who have been at each others' throats for centuries.

In peacetime, when armies train on assault courses where live ammunition is fired only a few inches above them, there are yearly casualties. The British Army accepts accidental deaths on these exercises of up to two per cent, without ordering a Court of Inquiry. By what bizarre logic or military mathematics this figure was arrived at is not clear.

In 1971, when a battalion of the Parachute Regiment was doing advanced infantry training on the Brecon Beacons, a Live Firing Attack was on the programme. According to a member of the battalion, 'To simulate battle, staff fired bullets over our heads and around our feet. It was a part of our training that everyone looked forward to with apprehension.'

At 0800 hrs an attack began on a cottage on the floor of a valley. Two men went left and set up a machine gun, with which they 'laid down a good pulse of supporting fire'. The attacking section moved down the gorse-covered hillside in pairs, one giving covering fire while the other 'danced and zig-zagged'. The narrator, who was at the machine gun, says, 'I noticed the advancing men getting dangerously near the arc of fire'. He moved the gun barrel a few degrees away from them.

A whistle blew and the order to cease fire was given. He could see the captain in charge of the exercise, a sergeant and a corporal 'running headlong down the hillside'. A camouflaged figure lay writhing at the valley bottom. The wounded paratrooper died a few hours later. Hit in the armpit and lung, he choked on his own blood.

Ballistics experts examined the bullet and proved that it had been fired by the captain.

Soon after this, the men who had taken part in the exercise were posted to Northern Ireland. The Battalion was shortly relieved by the Royal Marines. One night two Marine patrols mistook each other for the IRA, shots were exchanged and a Marine was killed.

The United States Navy has made some unfortunate misidentifications in recent times. In 1988 an echo on the radar aboard *USS Vincennes* was thought to be from a hostile aircraft – which was promptly shot down. It was an Iranian Airlines Airbus carrying 290 passengers, all of whom and the crew perished.

In 1992, during NATO war games in the Aegean, the United States aircraft carrier *Saratoga* fired two Sea Sparrow anti-aircraft missiles. One hit the bridge of a Turkish destroyer, killed the captain and four other officers and wounded fifteen ratings. Admiral Kelso, Chief of US Naval Operations, refused to accept that human error was necessarily to blame, although experts considered a technical fault to be virtually impossible. According to an expert on the staff of *Jane's Defence Weekly*, 'The best educated guess is that someone pushed the button when they should not have done.' If we substitute 'he' for 'they', we have an even better-educated guess – at least, a grammatical one.

The factors that contribute to attacking a friend in mistake for the enemy are easy to identify but not so easy to eliminate. The first is terrain: whether the country is wooded and allows concealment, or open. The second is weather: poor visibility in rain, mist, dust storms. The third is the type of operation: rapid movement, heavy supporting fire, patrolling, are all more productive of blue on blue than static warfare. The fourth is modern technology, which has produced weapons of great range and increased lethality. The fifth is carelessness, the human element that will never be eradicated. The sixth is battle fatigue: under stress even experienced surgeons make fatal mistakes, let alone soldiers, sailors and airmen.

These preliminaries bring us to the Gulf War and the deaths resulting from amicidal incidents. There were twenty-eight of these in which thirty-five American troops were killed and seventy-two wounded – twenty-three per cent of the total 615 battle casualties. Of United States Army combat vehicles lost, seventy-seven per cent were attributable to the same cause – seven Abrams tanks out of seven, and twenty Bradley fighting vehicles out of twenty-five.

There were four occasions when, altogether, nine British soldiers were killed and sixteen injured. Their deaths at the hands of United States Air Force pilots caused the greatest frenzy of complaints and demands for reparation and retribution. That attitude prompted this book. The conclusions of the Board of Inquiry into the British deaths and injuries are therefore quoted below, as reported to the House of Commons by the Minister for the Armed Forces in July, 1991.

'The Board of Inquiry into the incident when nine soldiers were killed and eleven injured in two Warrior vehicles belonging to the 3rd Battalion The Royal Regiment of Fusiliers Battle Group (3RRF) has now been reported. It has not been the practice of successive Governments to publish reports of this kind, but I wish to give as full an account as possible of the Board's findings.

'On 26 February, 1991, 3RRF had fought their way through a number of enemy positions in southern Iraq. After a brief but intense sandstorm during the early part of the advance, the weather had improved to give clear skies and good visibility by about 1500 hours local time, when C Company 3RRF, with some 37 Warrior and Engineer vehicles was reorganizing. The terrain in the area was flat and featureless apart from some Iraqi defensive positions and abandoned vehicles and equipment. During the reorganization, Royal Engineers prepared to destroy nearby Iraqi artillery pieces. When the demolition charges were about to be blown, C Company Commander instructed his men to re-enter their vehicles, close hatches and move away from the gun emplacements.

'8 Platoon had been stationary and out of their vehicles for about 15 minutes before this order was given. As they started to comply, one Warrior, callsign 22, exploded. Another Warrior, callsign 23, immediately manoeuvred in front of callsign 22, and some crew members had just begun to move the casualties to the first aid post when callsign 23 also exploded. A-10 aircraft were seen in the area at the time of the explosion, but at first mines were suspected.

'Earlier during the day, two successive flights of United States Air Force (USAF) aircraft were tasked by Headquarters 1st (British) Armoured Division to attack Iraqi armour at grid reference PT6857. Subsequently, a further flight of two USAF A-10 aircraft reported for tasking to the British Assistant Divisional Air Liaison Officer (DALO). His intention was that these aircraft should attack the same target as the two previous flights but there is a conflict of evidence over whether a grid reference for the target was passed from the Assistant DALO to the A-10s. The target location was over 20km to the east of C Company 3RRF's position at 1500 hours.

'The A-10 pilots identified what they thought was the target area from a physical description given them by a departing USAF F-16 of the previous flight, and shortly afterwards saw what they thought were about 50 Iraqi T54/55 tanks and support vehicles heading north. The pilots had been told that there were no friendly forces within 10 kilometres of their target, and these vehicles were closer than that to the point they had identified as their target. The lead aircraft made two passes, at 15,000 and 8,000 feet, to observe the vehicles with binoculars, but saw no friendly markings. Both aircraft then fired one infra-red Maverick missile from a height of about 9,000 feet, each destroying one of the vehicles, before reporting the engagement to the Assistant DALO and leaving the area.

'The pilots' report of 50 Iraqi vehicles differed so dramatically from earlier descriptions of the target that the Assistant DALO asked them to confirm the location. The flight leader reported that the attack had taken place at grid reference PT 418518. The Assistant DALO immediately realized that this position was more than 20 kilometres from the intended target and corresponded with the location of 3RRF. He then called up a reconnaissance flight over the area, which reported that fluorescent air recognition panels could be seen from 6,000 feet and the type of vehicles could be identified from 14,000 feet.

'The Board of Inquiry found that 8 Platoon, C Company 3RRF were on operations as ordered. The Board also found that the air planning procedures allowing a distance of more than 15 kilometres between the target for any attack and friendly forces had been followed and should have been sufficient to ensure the successful and safe conduct of operations. The Board further concluded that air control at Corps and Divisional level which provided tasking information to the A-10s was in accordance with established procedures.

'The Board found that 8 Platoon's vehicles were displaying correct inverted V recognition signals and fluorescent panels. The Board noted that some of the panels could have been partially obscured by open hatches or equipment, and that while a reconnaissance flight observed the panels at 6,000 feet, this was below the operating height of the A-10s. The Board could not make any finding as to whether the pilots should have seen the identification panels at their operating height.

'The Board concluded that no blame or responsibility for the incident could be attributed to 3RRF.

'The Board noted that there was a conflict of evidence between the statements of the witnesses from Headquarters 1st (British) Armoured Division and those of the A-10 pilots. The Assistant DALO stated that he passed the target grid reference but the A-10 pilots deny receiving this. There was no evidence to suggest that the two previous missions had attacked anything but the correct targets. On the evidence presented, the Board found that no blame or responsibility should be attached to the Assistant DALO.

'The pilots stated that, notwithstanding the absence of a grid reference, they attacked on the basis of information passed to them by the previous flight and of their positive identification of the targets as enemy vehicles. The Board noted that a USAF reconnaissance flight shortly after the Warriors were attacked was able to identify the types of vehicles from 14,000 feet. On the basis of the evidence before it, the Board was unable to establish why the attacked Warrior vehicles were misidentified by the A-10 pilots as enemy T54/55 tanks, particularly in view of their previous identification runs at 8,000 feet and 15,000 feet. In forwarding the Board's findings, the Joint Commander has drawn attention to the way in which aspect, weather and light conditions can critically affect a pilot's ability to identify the details of objects on the ground.

'The Board did not establish whether the USAF personnel involved were at fault. It was clearly established that the USAF A-10s delivered the missiles, but the Board could not establish precisely why they attacked the wrong target.

'The Board remarked that it was clear that all UK and USAF personnel involved were striving to achieve their individual tasks to the best of their abilities in a fast-moving battle. The Board thought it inevitable that, at some stage, difficulties may arise when individuals are under pressure. On 26 February, 1991, difficulties arose in relation to the location and identification of the target, and the Board concluded that only the clearest of standard operating procedures and sophisticated identification systems will help to prevent such tragedies in the future.

'The Board recommended that a study be initiated to identify a suitable air recognition system for future use, confirmed the importance of standard operating procedure for the control of aircraft in offensive air support operations and recommended that they must always include instructions that a grid reference or a latitude and longitude is specifically included in mission briefs and that this is always acknowledged by the pilots.

'The Government (and the United States Administration) wish to express their deepest sympathy and condolences to relatives of those who died in this tragic incident.

'During the conflict there were a further three incidents involving friendly fire in which British Servicemen were injured.

'The first of these occurred shortly after 1100 local time on 26 February. An officer attached to 1 Staffords received shrapnel wounds when a Warrior vehicle was attacked by a Challenger tank of the Scots Dragoon Guards. Personnel from 1 Staffords were guarding prisoners of war when a Challenger tank from the Scots Dragoon Guards began to engage nearby Iraqi armoured vehicles, which later turned out to be abandoned. The tank mistakenly fired on the vehicles of 1 Staffords, hitting the Warrior, before moving off. Visibility at the time was reduced by a dust storm to about 400 metres. All the Staffords' vehicles were marked with the inverted V device and carried orange fluorescent panels. The four personnel in the Warrior were unharmed, but shrapnel injured an officer who had dismounted from another vehicle. Once the mistake was realized, the Scots Dragoon Guards returned to the scene and evacuated the officer to hospital.

'Another incident occurred shortly after 1100 local time on 27 February. Two personnel from the Queen's Royal Irish Hussars (QRIH) were injured when their Scorpion armoured reconnaissance vehicles were fired on by US M1 Abrams tanks. Both Scorpions were carrying the black inverted V device and visibility was good. UK and US forces had their own areas of operations and the QRIH Section was about 2 kilometres within its area. They had stopped to take the surrender of Iraqi troops, when one Scorpion was hit in the front by a round from a US M1 tank, firing from about 1,500 metres to the North. The driver escaped without injury, but a soldier walking alongside received shrapnel wounds. The other Scorpion came under tank and machine-gun fire, the soldier manning the turret-mounted machine gun also received shrapnel wounds. When the US personnel realized their mistake they assisted with the treatment of the injured British soldiers and their evacuation to hospital.

'The third incident also occurred on 27 February. At about 1445 local time, two soldiers from 10 Air Defence Battery, Royal Artillery, received burns when two Spartan armoured cars from which they had dismounted were engaged by Challenger tanks from 14/20 Hussars with thermal sights beyond the range of unaided visibility (about 1,500 metres). In these conditions, it was not possible to identify the inverted V device carried by the vehicles. The rearmost vehicle was hit and burst into flames. The other vehicle was also damaged in the ensuing fire. The Spartan destroyed was empty and was being towed after breaking down. The Spartans had become detached from a convoy of 7th Armoured Brigade vehicles which had been delayed in getting clear of the area because of the difficult terrain.'

Nobody who is not the pilot or navigator of a fast jet military aeroplane knows what is involved in making a decision to fire when you must do it, not visually, but from map references, while flying at several hundred miles an hour and many miles from the target when you have to release your missiles.

General Schwarzkopf is no mere theoretician. He is a seasoned fighting soldier with a distinguished combat record in Vietnam. His words on the subject are wise and sober: 'The very chaotic nature of the battlefield, where quick decisions make the difference between life and death, has resulted in numerous incidents of troops being killed by their own side in every war that has ever been fought. This does not make it acceptable. Not even one such avoidable death should ever be considered acceptable.'

In the Gulf War certain conditions prevailed for the first time. The Allies' technological ability to engage targets exceeded their ability to identify targets clearly. For years they had been working on the ability to attack enemy targets at great ranges to destroy as many of them as possible before they themselves were engaged by the enemy. It was possible to introduce a means of identifying friendly forces from enemy, but this would also have enabled the enemy to make the same discrimination. The distance at which a decision to shoot had to be taken was made greater when it was found that the desert environment enhanced the ability to acquire and engage targets at a great range.

Vehement protests and demands for financial 'compensation' echoed around the world. Such a display of moral outrage was unprecedented. It happened for two reasons. The fighting was contained in so small an area and the multitude of reporters belonging to the world's press, radio and television organizations were concentrated physically in place and mentally on a few days of battle. In other wars it had been possible to screen ugly events. In this one it was not.

This was a war when every military action was under arc lights and viewed by a myriad journalists who had the means of instant communication with the whole world.

Half a century earlier and in a war that encompassed most of the world, concealment had been possible. When a Spitfire shot down a Harvard over Burma in 1945, the offending squadron's Operational Record Book entry, of which copies had to be sent to higher formations all the way up to the Air Ministry, easily camouflaged the accident. 'On this patrol of the Ywadon area, Blue 1 and 2 saw three aircraft flying North to South at approx 500 ft. The third aircraft, a radial-engined machine, appeared to be making an attack on the other two aircraft which were identified as Hurricanes. Blue Leader went in to attack the radial-engined machine and opened fire just before recognizing it as a Harvard. The Harvard force landed in a field and the crew of two were uninjured.'

The Hurricanes were a fabrication; and, as the reader knows, both men in the Harvard were wounded.

Autres temps, autres moeurs. But it is not the behaviour or morality that have changed, it is the means and speed of communication. What will never change, however, is the fact that friendly fire still happens and always will. Also, when it is feasible, those who were guilty and, where possible, their seniors in their Services, will do all they can to obfuscate the facts – at least for public propagation.

INDEX

Malmédy. USAAF bomb it
in error three times, 131–132
Markham, Rear Admiral A. See
HMS Camperdown
McKellar, Squadron Leader A.A.,
DSO, DFC, (and bar), shoots
down Hampden, 58
Minesweepers. See Sea, accidents at
Monte Cassino. USAAF bomb
British and Indian troops
and Italian civilians, 111–114
Mortars. RAF on ground training
under fire from own Motor
Gunboats. See Sea, accidents at.

New Zealand Army. See Gallipoli
Night fighter, USAAF, shoots at
and misses RAF night fighter but
claims a victory, 117; RAF night
fighter shoots down Mosquito
and claims it was a Ju188, 119
Normandy. USAAF bombs
American troops, 123; USAAF
does it again next day, 124;
USAAF bombs Canadian and
Polish troops, 125; Canadian
squadrons in RAF bomb own
troops, 125, 126; RAF pilot bales
out of Typhoon, Germans put
him in lorry which a Typhoon
shoots up, 126; Typhoon pilot
shot down is put in German
ambulance which is strafed by
RAF, 126, 127; RAF and USAAF
strafe Canadians and Poles, who
shoot back, 127. Typhoons
constantly attacked by USAAF
fighters and occasionally by RAF
fighters, 133.
North Africa, 75, 76
Nurput Sing. See Indian Mutiny

Oxspring, Group Captain R.H.
'Bobby', DFC, AFC, describes

inability of USAAF fighter
pilots in North Africa to identify
friendly fighters from enemy, 96

Palestine. Attacks by Jewish
terrorist gangs on British troops
and Arab civilians. When country
became Israel, attacks by Israeli
Army on Arab civilians, 143–147
Polish pilot, shot down over
London, mistaken for German
is lynched by civilians, 71–72
Portuguese Army. As allies of
British, go into Front Line in
Great War. They bolt under
attack and are fired upon by
British, 50–52

Roodamow. See Indian Mutiny
Rooya. See Indian Mutiny
Rose, Pilot Officer F.C., shot down
by Spitfires, 9, 12
Royal Flying Corps under friendly
fire, 53

St Nazaire, naval attack on.
Germans fire on own vessel and
RAF hit British destroyer with
bomb, 87–89
Salisbury Plain.
Demonstration of ground
strafing, one fighter shoots up
spectators, 77
Salerno. American troops shoot
one another and at British, 107
USS *Saratoga* hits Turkish
destroyer, 149, 150
Sari Bair. See Gallipoli
Schwarzkopf, General Norman. On
subject of 'friendly fire', 2, 155
Sea, accidents at. Evacuating troops
from Dunkirk on moonless night,
British vessels in conflict and
collision with loss of life, 64, 65;
Polish destroyer off course sunk

by British destroyer, 86; Motor
Gunboat Flotilla from Lowestoft
attacked by MGB Flotilla from
Yarmouth, officer and rating
killed, 89; Minesweeper off
North African coast attacked
by German bomber, rating in
minesweeper accidentally wounds
his captain, 90; acting on orders
given on wrong information from
navy, Typhoons are compelled
to attack minesweepers that are
British, not German. Heavy loss
of naval lives One of the greatest
tragedies of the war, 128–130
HMS Sheffield attacked by Fleet Air
Arm Swordfish, 85
Sicily. British and American
parachute and glider-borne troops
attacking Gela and Primosole
Bridge are fired on by own
ships, tanks and artillery, 98–101
Souk el Arba (Tunisia). British
paratroops killed and injured
when they jumped from too low,
because meteorologists did not
warn of thin air, 98
South African troops bombed by
RAF, 4

Tanks. Amphibious ones sink on
D-day when launched far from
beach, 118
Tanks. British and American
tanks operating together wipe
out four British tanks that they
misidentify, 138
Thousand-bomber raids, introduce
danger of high-flying bombers
hitting friendly aircraft flying
beneath. This often happens, 106
Tryon, Admiral Sir George.
Gives order that causes his
flagship, *HMS Victoria*, to ram
and sink *HMS Camperdown*, 38

Tuck, Wing Commander R.S.,
DFC (and two bars), shoots
down German bomber that
lands on hut and kills his
brother-in-law, 61

HMS Victoria sinks *HMS
Camperdown*, 38
USS *Vincennes* shoots down Iranian
Airbus, 149
Wapping. Civilians lynch
shot-down Polish pilot, thinking
him German, 71

Zürich bombed by USAAF, 139